S. Hrg. 113–362

SOLDIERS AS CONSUMERS: PREDATORY AND UNFAIR BUSINESS PRACTICES HARMING THE MILITARY COMMUNITY

HEARING

BEFORE THE

COMMITTEE ON COMMERCE, SCIENCE, AND TRANSPORTATION UNITED STATES SENATE

ONE HUNDRED THIRTEENTH CONGRESS

FIRST SESSION

NOVEMBER 20, 2013

Printed for the use of the Committee on Commerce, Science, and Transportation

U.S. GOVERNMENT PRINTING OFFICE

89–464 PDF WASHINGTON : 2014

For sale by the Superintendent of Documents, U.S. Government Printing Office
Internet: bookstore.gpo.gov Phone: toll free (866) 512–1800; DC area (202) 512–1800
Fax: (202) 512–2104 Mail: Stop IDCC, Washington, DC 20402–0001

SENATE COMMITTEE ON COMMERCE, SCIENCE, AND TRANSPORTATION

ONE HUNDRED THIRTEENTH CONGRESS

FIRST SESSION

JOHN D. ROCKEFELLER IV, West Virginia, *Chairman*

BARBARA BOXER, California	JOHN THUNE, South Dakota, *Ranking*
BILL NELSON, Florida	ROGER F. WICKER, Mississippi
MARIA CANTWELL, Washington	ROY BLUNT, Missouri
MARK PRYOR, Arkansas	MARCO RUBIO, Florida
CLAIRE McCASKILL, Missouri	KELLY AYOTTE, New Hampshire
AMY KLOBUCHAR, Minnesota	DEAN HELLER, Nevada
MARK WARNER, Virginia	DAN COATS, Indiana
MARK BEGICH, Alaska	TIM SCOTT, South Carolina
RICHARD BLUMENTHAL, Connecticut	TED CRUZ, Texas
BRIAN SCHATZ, Hawaii	DEB FISCHER, Nebraska
EDWARD MARKEY, Massachusetts	RON JOHNSON, Wisconsin
CORY BOOKER, New Jersey	

ELLEN L. DONESKI, *Staff Director*
JAMES REID, *Deputy Staff Director*
JOHN WILLIAMS, *General Counsel*
DAVID SCHWIETERT, *Republican Staff Director*
NICK ROSSI, *Republican Deputy Staff Director*
REBECCA SEIDEL, *Republican General Counsel and Chief Investigator*

CONTENTS

	Page
Hearing held on November 20, 2013	1
Statement of Senator Rockefeller	1
Statement of Senator Thune	3
Prepared statement of the American Financial Services Association	5
Statement of Senator Nelson	9
Statement of Senator Ayotte	46
Statement of Senator Markey	48

WITNESSES

Hon. Robert E. Cooper, Jr., Attorney General, State of Tennessee	9
Prepared statement	12
Hollister K. Petraeus, Assistant Director, Consumer Financial Protection Bureau, Office of Servicemember Affairs	15
Prepared statement	17
Charles Harwood, Deputy Director, Federal Trade Commission's Bureau of Consumer Protection	23
Prepared statement	25
Deanna R. Nelson, Assistant Attorney General In Charge (Watertown Regional), State of New York, Office of Attorney General Eric T. Schneiderman	31
Prepared statement	33
Dwain Alexander II, Senior Civilian Attorney, Region Legal Service Office, Mid-Atlantic, U.S. Navy	36
Prepared statement	38

APPENDIX

Michael S. Archer, prepared statement	57
National Independent Automobile Dealers Association (NIADA), prepared statement	64
Response to written questions submitted by Hon. Amy Klobuchar to Deanna R. Nelson	66

SOLDIERS AS CONSUMERS: PREDATORY AND UNFAIR BUSINESS PRACTICES HARMING THE MILITARY COMMUNITY

WEDNESDAY, NOVEMBER 20, 2013

U.S. SENATE,
COMMITTEE ON COMMERCE, SCIENCE, AND TRANSPORTATION,
Washington, DC.

The Committee met, pursuant to notice, at 2:35 p.m. in room SR–253, Russell Senate Office Building, Senator John D. Rockefeller IV, Chairman of the Committee, presiding.

OPENING STATEMENT OF HON. JOHN D. ROCKEFELLER IV, U.S. SENATOR FROM WEST VIRGINIA

The CHAIRMAN. The tall man has come.
[Laughter.]
Senator THUNE. That's you.
The CHAIRMAN. No, that's you. And the hearing is called to order.
This month, we—and this is a subject which I want to dive deeply into. This will not be the only hearing. There are scoundrels out there and they have to be uncovered and whatever one does next.
This month, we celebrate Veteran's Day and the remarkable men and women who make extraordinary sacrifices protecting our country. As we honor the service and the bravery they have shown in conflicts across the world, we should remember their challenges on the home front as well. Thus begins my statement.
Like the rest of us, our soldiers, airmen, sailors, and marines are consumers and young ones at that. Not experienced ones at that, for the most part. And vulnerable to consumer practices at that, for the most part. They buy homes; they buy cars, computers, and other products essential to maintaining a household.
We're going to learn today their steady paychecks and relative job security make our servicewomen and men appealing targets for unscrupulous businesses—I've got other words I'd like to use; pitching predatory loan products. Holly Petraeus, you know all about this. That's not something any of us should be proud of but it is the fact. I'm not sure that this has been dealt with in any committee before, but it's going to be dealt one in this one and at length.
One of the essential promises we make to those who put their lives on the line to protect our freedom is that we will, in turn, honor their service when they are at home. To uphold this pledge we must make sure that we understand the unique challenges they face when they act as consumers and that their special role in our

society may require some special protections, whether that's regulations or whether that's laws, remains to be seen.

Rigorous training requirements and the relative isolation of some bases can make it tough for our military servicemen to comparison shop for goods and financing options. Frequent moves demanded by the job, which can include months on end in war zones, hence their victims overseas as well as here, can make tracking bills and negotiating with debt collectors virtually impossible.

Beyond that, our soldiers, airmen, sailors, and marines may also be particularly vulnerable to aggressive debt collection techniques. For example, many members of the military need security clearances to perform their jobs. We have heard reports about unscrupulous debt collectors who, in violation of Federal law, threaten to put military servicemembers' security clearances at risk by disclosing their debts to their commanding officers. Well, bravo, for those wonderful little companies that choose to do that.

Today, we're going to explore financial issues affecting the economic well-being of military households practicing involving small dollar loan products that carry extremely high long-term costs and aggressive debt collection tactics our servicemen may face when bills come due.

Many families across the country face emergency expenses and times when their monthly budgets just don't cover it all. There are a variety of lenders that want to help. They offer their products to help them bridge those financial moments and gaps. Then it becomes a very different story; however, when these products involve predatory components such as egregiously high interest rates, which in some cases top 300 percent, high fees or waivers of sudden rights hidden in fine print of contracts. We got familiar with that with the health insurance industry, or other unfair or deceptive tactics. And it's particularly troubling when lenders use geographic proximity to military bases and target advertising techniques to encourage members of the military to enter into these predatory loans.

These are young people for the most part. Some of the more common small dollar, high cost loan products advertised, specifically to military members that I've heard about, include the following: payday loans, which take repayment from the borrower's next paycheck and carry annual percentage rates of 200–300 percent; installment loans for cash or retail items, like electronics whose interests and fees ultimately can total more than the original price of the goods; and auto title lending, where the loan is secured by title to a consumer's car in which gives lenders leverage to increase loan rates under the threat of repossession of the car. We've dealt with that in this committee, not so much on servicemembers, but when people move and they hire a moving van and the bank comes and picks up all their stuff, and then the van goes ten miles down the road and pulls onto an off-road and phones them and saying, "I'm sorry, we didn't charge what we were meant to. You either pay us or we're out of here." It's a lovely world.

Other concerning practices include various deceptive schemes used to cell automobiles to our service men and women. One example of a recent predatory scheme targeting military members was uncovered by one of our witnesses today, Tennessee Attorney General Robert Cooper. General Cooper will discuss in more detail his inquiry showed that electronics retailer, SmartBuy, which stores on the outskirts of military bases, pushed installment loans of consumer products such as computers to military members at inflated rates through deceptive tactics such as undisclosed fees and high interest rates.

Despite protections in state and Federal laws, consumer advocates report that military servicemen are still being harmed by these predatory practices. One recent news account highlighted the case of a marine staff sergeant who took out an auto title loan for $1,600 and not realizing that the fine print of the contract required him to pay back more than $17,000 over two and a half years. So, obviously, he fell behind in his payments and his car was repossessed and sold at auction. How we honor our servicemen and women.

A Federal law called the Military Lending Act is supposed to protect servicemembers from this kind of abuse, but did not appear to apply in this case because MLA only covers loans with a term of 6 months or less. This is clearly a loophole that needs to be closed.

Today, we're going to learn about more trends in unfair and predatory business practices from a group of individuals who are leading the charge to promote consumer protection for our military. They have been working very hard, the group of folks in front of me, to promote partnerships among consumer advocates at the base, state, and Federal level. And I hope that the testimony today will help inform us about the best ways that we can possibly do to build on these efforts.

Our military is always prepared to give full measure. That is our soldiers. We owe them the same when it comes to protecting them from unscrupulous practices at home. And I just want to say, unnecessarily but necessary to me, I spent 10 years in the Veterans' Committee trying to prove, but finally successfully, that when the Department of Defense, not necessarily looking after these folks that I'm talking about, doing something called the Gulf War syndrome. You may remember it. Soldiers, sailors, and other who were in Iraq were told to take something called "pyridostigmine bromide" which had not been cleared by the FDA, even for animals. They were forced to take it by our DOD every single day and tens and tens and tens of thousands, hundreds of thousands of people couldn't sleep; broke out in rashes; they couldn't read a newspaper; their marriages broke up, and the DOD continually refused to say that it was their fault or that there was any problem. And ten years later, no thanks to DOD, they admitted that they had been wrong.

The distinguished Ranking Member, Senator Thune, from the urban state of South Dakota.

STATEMENT OF HON. JOHN THUNE, U.S. SENATOR FROM SOUTH DAKOTA

Senator THUNE. Thank you, Mr. Chairman, for holding this hearing to examine unfair financial practices that may be harming our military community; it's something that I'm sure all of us, as members of this committee, care about. And I also want to thank our witnesses for being here today to testify.

South Dakota is home to Ellsworth Air Force Base where there are more than 9,000 military personnel, family members, and civilian employees. In addition, there are 4,250 Air Guard and Army Guard members who serve in my home state. I'm proud of their courage and grateful for their sacrifice and service to our country. I certainly do not want to see them or their families subjected to unfair financial practices.

This hearing will highlight the types of unfair practices and financial fraud that may be targeting our military men and women; the education and the assistance programs available; and the law enforcement efforts undertaken to eliminate the worse practices and scams.

Servicemembers, like all consumers, are not immune to the problems encountered by taking on too much debt. However, the unique demands of military service may exacerbate the negative consequences from too much debt.

For servicemembers, unlike ordinary consumers, failing to pay any kind of debt is considered an offense under the Uniform Code of Military Justice, which could lead to a loss of a security clearance or even result in administrative discharge.

Admiral Mike Mullen, then Chief of Naval Operations, was quoted voicing strong concerns about these issues in a June 2006 article of *Sea Power* where he stated and I quote, "A sailor's financial readiness directly impacts unit readiness and the navy's ability to accomplish its mission." As mentioned in the article, financial difficulties were the number one reason that sailors were losing their security clearance and this was affecting the availability of servicemembers for overseas deployments.

Due to the efforts of Senators Jim Talent and Bill Nelson, Congress took notice of those challenges and enacted the Military Lending Act in 2006, which is an important step in protecting against predatory lenders. While that law has largely been a success, the Department of Defense is currently considering whether its rule implementing the Military Lending Act needs to be updated.

The Department of Defense takes the issue of financial readiness seriously. I appreciate that the department has made great strides to enhance its education training and counseling by beginning financial training right from the start, during basic training, and continuing throughout the servicemember's career.

As the issue of whether further solutions are warranted is examined, it is important to ensure that there's proper balance with access to appropriate credit while also protecting servicemembers from unfair practices and outright fraud.

I hope we can use this hearing today to highlight the financial assistance and education efforts that are available to servicemembers to make informed decisions and to protect against fraud. For instance, the military has legal assistance offices that offer financial education counseling. I look forward to hearing from Captain Alexander, who serves in the Navy's mid-Atlantic Regional Legal Service Office, about his role in supporting and advising servicemembers when they fall victim to financial fraud.

I also look forward to hearing more about the consumer protection initiative from the Federal Trade Commission and the Consumer Financial Protection Bureau. We're privileged to have Mrs. Holly Petraeus here today to tell us of her efforts with the Office of Servicemember Affairs at the CFPB. I know that she has visited personally with the servicemembers stationed at Ellsworth, as well as dozens of other military installations.

I'd also like to call attention to Military Consumer Protection Day which was held for the first time this past July. Its website provides education and resources to servicemembers and their families to protect them against fraud.

In closing, we can all agree that financial readiness is an important issue for our military and our national security, and that these brave men and women that protect all over the world should not be the victims of unfair practices at home.

So Mr. Chairman, I thank you again for holding this hearing and I look forward to hearing from our witnesses and what certain states are doing to rein in unscrupulous practices. I would ask too, I have a statement here by the American Financial Services Association, that I'd like to have included as part of the record.

[The information referred to follows:]

PREPARED STATEMENT OF THE AMERICAN FINANCIAL SERVICES ASSOCIATION

Statement of Interest

The American Financial Services Association ("AFSA") is pleased to file these comments to the Senate Commerce Committee on the occasion of its hearing on "Soldiers as Consumers: Predatory and Unfair Business Practices Harming the Military Community."

AFSA is the national trade association for the consumer credit industry, protecting access to credit and consumer choice. The association encourages and maintains ethical business practices and supports financial education for consumers of all ages. AFSA has provided services to its members for over 95 years. AFSA's 350 member companies include consumer and commercial finance companies, vehicle finance companies including the captives, credit card issuers, mortgage lenders, industrial banks, and other financial service firms that lend to consumers and small businesses.

AFSA member companies offer many types of consumer credit products, including credit cards, vehicle loans and leases, personal installment loans and mortgages (together hereinafter referred to as "consumer installment credit"). AFSA members are responsible for providing roughly 80 percent of the Nation's vehicle financing. In general, finance companies represent one of every five dollars of consumer credit outstanding.

AFSA is very appreciative of the Committee's desire to examine the financial issues and concerns faced by military servicemembers and their families. We are sensitive to the hardship that is placed on military families with repeated deployments, especially for dual career spouses, and the financial difficulties created by frequent moves.

AFSA works continuously with regulators at the state and Federal levels to ensure that servicemembers and their families are protected against unscrupulous lending practices.

AFSA Members Strive to Understand and Meet the Needs of Servicemembers and their Families

AFSA members serve servicemembers and their families by offering beneficial forms of consumer installment credit, which:

- Have existed for over a hundred years;
- Are based on the borrower's ability to pay;
- Are paid in equal monthly installments of principal and interest like traditional mortgages, which give borrowers a roadmap out of debt; and
- Are fully regulated by Federal and state laws, and the Federal and state agencies empowered to enforce those laws.

Additionally, AFSA members report to the credit bureaus to allow responsible borrowers to improve their credit score, and provide a number of financial literacy programs including the AFSA Educational Foundation's ("AFSAEF") MoneySKILL program.

AFSA members endeavor to provide the best customer service to all of their customers, including servicemembers and their families. We always attempt to assist all of our customers, servicemembers and civilians alike, in times of hardship and inconvenience to work out financial solutions to their problems. We realize that condoning harmful lending practices to servicemembers and their families endangers the good actors in the lending industry. We strive to comply with all regulations and statutes, including the Military Lending Act and the Servicemembers Civil Relief Act.

It is imperative to ensure that servicemembers and their families have access to a full range of legitimate and fair credit opportunities. Burdensome restrictions on legitimate practices serve to limit the range of financial products that are available to servicemembers and their families. This reduces competition and moves counter to the objective of empowering servicemembers and their families.

The key to protecting servicemembers and their families is transparency—simple, clear, plain-language disclosures and terms that are fair, without tricks or traps. Finance companies use plain-language disclosures for servicemembers and civilian borrowers alike. Along these lines, AFSA members' practices include: (1) letting the borrower see the cost of the loan in simple terms; and (2) if ancillary products are offered by the lender, such as credit insurance, providing a clear statement of the cost and the optional nature of these products, and obtaining affirmative consent if the consumer chooses to purchase them.

We want servicemembers and their families to continue to have access to affordable, safe and disciplined consumer installment credit. AFSA is willing to meet with the entire military chain of command to inform them about our members' financial products and seek their advice on additional guidelines that may be needed to encourage even better lending practices. We are also eager to work with the Department of Defense ("DOD") and the military branches to support efforts on financial education.

AFSA hopes to be a resource to the Consumer Financial Protection Bureau's ("CFPB") Office of Servicemember Affairs in order to encourage standards of ethics and ensure that servicemembers and their families are not targeted by unfair lending practices. Leveraging our industry's resources can increase the ability of the CFPB to ensure that servicemembers and their families are treated fairly.

Occasionally, concerns about potentially abusive practices are brought to the attention of AFSA and its members. Whether these concerns relate to civilian or military consumers, we take such matters very seriously. AFSA members strive to respond promptly to individual customer complaints as soon as they are made aware of them. However, oftentimes generalized observations are made about lending practices based upon anecdotal examples that do not represent industry norms. Furthermore, observations relating to certain types of short-term credit products that AFSA members do not offer have sometimes been applied to traditional installment loans, which, as discussed below, carry significantly different features. Traditional installment loans are underwritten strictly based upon the borrower's ability to repay and they are structured under a more disciplined debt reduction schedule than the newer hyper-lending products—which have been where problems have arisen for servicemembers who become trapped in a cycle of debt.

In general, the rare cases of alleged illegal behavior could, and should, be addressed under existing consumer protection statutes and regulations, or the criminal code, at the state and Federal levels. Where there is empirical data to support a pattern or practice of such behavior, AFSA and its members are extremely interested to know about it so that we may take steps proactively to address shortcomings in compliance with the law.

Defense Department Regulation Protects Military Community from Risky Forms of Credit

In 2006, Congress enacted provisions in Section 670 of the John Warner National Defense Authorization Act for Fiscal Year 2007 (commonly known as the "Military Lending Act" or "MLA") to cap the annual percentage rate ("APR") at 36 percent and impose other limitations on certain consumer loans to servicemembers and their dependents, with the objective of protecting military households from becoming trapped in a cycle of debt.[1]

---

[1] 10 *USC* 987. Terms of Consumer Credit Extended to Members and Dependents: Limitations. Public Law 109–364. October 17, 2006.

Implementing regulations promulgated by the DOD in 2007 ("Final Rule") contain limitations on and requirements for certain types of consumer credit extended to covered borrowers—which include active-duty servicemembers and their spouses, children and other dependents. The Final Rule applies to payday loans, vehicle title loans and tax refund anticipation loans.[2]

DOD Rule Sufficiently Protects Servicemembers and their Families

In its only report following the issuance of the Final Rule, the DOD itself said that the rule is achieving its intended purpose.[3]

Assessing the effectiveness of the Final Rule, Col. Paul Kantwill, Director of Legal Policy in the Office of the Under Secretary of Defense (Personnel & Readiness), stated the following in his June 2012 testimony to the Senate Banking Committee:[4]

> With the assistance of the seven Federal financial regulatory agencies, DOD was able to draft and release a regulation within the prescribed time limitation seen as acceptable and workable by both the consumer advocates and the mainstream financial industry providers. . . Annually, the Department has sent a representative to the national conference of state regulators to ensure there are no difficulties in obtaining compliance from the covered creditors. Each year the regulators have reported that their examinations have found compliance with the Rule and no need for enforcement action.

At a November 2011 hearing, Admiral Steve Abbot, USN (Ret.), the President of the Navy-Marine Corps Relief Society, told the Banking Committee that "the Military Lending Act (MLA), which became effective in October 2007, has dramatically curtailed payday loans to active duty servicemembers." This would seem to suggest that existing statute is serving its purpose.[5]

Officials Warn of Unintended Consequences of Restricting Access to Credit

As Holly Petraeus, Assistant Director of the CFPB's Office of Servicemember Affairs, stated in her testimony at the very same hearing, it is imperative that any laws or regulations that policymakers may propose in the future do not result in unintended consequences.[6] The inadvertent risk of restricting the availability of legitimate and appropriate credit products to deserving servicemembers and their families would be far more devastating than most people recognize. It was this concern that prompted the DOD to limit the scope of the Final Rule to payday loans, vehicle title loans and tax refund anticipation loans.

Further, in responding to a question from a member of the Banking Committee, Mrs. Petraeus expressed concern about the unintended consequences of extending the existing 36 percent APR rate cap beyond the products covered by the Final Rule. AFSA shares that concern and urges policymakers to consider the consequences of regulating useful, desirable forms of consumer credit out of existence for the military community.

Finally, Defense Secretary Leon Panetta expressed satisfaction with current policy when he responded to a question posed by Sen. Vitter upon his June 2011 confirmation hearing about whether the Department saw a need to expand the scope of the regulation:[7]

> No, the DOD has not changed its policy and does not intend at this time to include other lenders within the coverage of the regulation. The Department proposes to help ensure that Service members and their families receive fair protections by working with Federal and state governments on existing and proposed policies impacting all consumers. The goal is to try to eliminate the need to identify Service members and their families for protections, which may create unintentional barriers to credit.

---

[2] 32 *CFR* 232. Limitations on Terms of Consumer Credit Extended to Service Members and Dependents; Final Rule. August 31, 2007.

[3] Department of Defense Report on Implementation of Limitations on Terms of Consumer Credit Extended to Service Members and Dependents. July 22, 2008.

[4] Kantwill, Col. Paul. Testimony before U.S. Senate Committee on Banking, Housing, and Urban Affairs, Hearing on "Empowering and Protecting Servicemembers, Veterans and their Families in the Consumer Financial Marketplace." June 26, 2012.

[5] Abbot, Admiral Steve, USN (Ret). Testimony before U.S. Senate Committee on Banking, Housing, and Urban Affairs, Hearing on "Empowering and Protecting Servicemembers, Veterans and their Families in the Consumer Financial Marketplace." November 3, 2011.

[6] Petraeus, Hollister K. Testimony before U.S. Senate Committee on Banking, Housing, and Urban Affairs, Hearing on "Empowering and Protecting Servicemembers, Veterans and their Families in the Consumer Financial Marketplace." November 3, 2011.

[7] Panetta, Hon. Leon E. Response to Questions for the Record submitted by Sen. David Vitter, Hearing before the U.S. Senate Committee on Armed Services. June 9, 2011.

AFSA notes that in the Final Rule, the DOD recognized the problems servicemembers and their families were facing from various new forms of harmful consumer credit and proposed regulations to protect them. The DOD saw the importance of implementing strong protections without unduly restricting access to valuable and beneficial traditional credit products for servicemembers and their dependents. AFSA agrees with the DOD that some newer forms of credit can be harmful to servicemembers, as detailed in the Department's 2006 report to Congress that motivated enactment of the MLA.[8] Payday loans, in particular, are a relatively new type of consumer credit, having originated and evolved primarily in recent years. By contrast, the consumer finance industry has been providing military servicemembers with fair and reasonably-priced access to credit in a safe and responsible manner for over a century in the form of traditional installment loans.

Policymakers should Tread Carefully before Restricting Credit to the Military

AFSA does not believe that further limiting access to credit for military households is wise or necessary at this juncture. To do so could create undue financial stress where none currently exists. Foreclosing upon the ability of servicemembers and their families to obtain traditional credit products could force them into the hands of non-traditional lenders—some of which are domiciled overseas and operate on the Internet, outside the reach of U.S. regulators—or even worse, underground and unregulated lenders (commonly known as "loan sharks"). Such a misstep would be detrimental to military personnel readiness, something that should be avoided at all costs.

The DOD understands the importance of maintaining access to beneficial credit as a compelling need for its personnel. In its Final Rule, the DOD notes "the potential for unintended consequences that could adversely affect credit availability if it were to adopt a broadly applicable regulation."[9] The DOD looked to identify the key problems and to use the authority granted by the MLA to define "consumer credit" in a way that achieves the intent of Congress while preserving the availability of beneficial forms of credit to military families.

Traditional Installment Loans

Installment Loans are Beneficial to Servicemembers and their Families

Traditional installment lending provides access to reasonably-priced credit because lenders work with borrowers to determine that they have the ability to repay the loan. It is the safest form of small-dollar lending. Installment loans utilize amortization as a means of protecting borrowers from an endless cycle of debt. The installment credit products offered by the member companies of AFSA are not the problem—in fact they are often the best solution to the financial needs of servicemembers and their families. Installment loans are clearly, and have long been, a beneficial and useful service for servicemembers and their families.

The beneficial features of installment loans were also recognized by the DOD in the conclusion of its report to Congress on the effectiveness of the regulations implementing the MLA: "Isolating detrimental credit products without impeding the availability of favorable installment loans was of central concern in developing the regulation. Consequently, installment loans that do not fit the definition of 'consumer credit' in Section 232.3(b). . .are not covered by the regulation."[10]

Conventional commercial banks, credit unions, and military relief societies are not in a position to provide adequate credit to servicemembers and their families due to the costs of underwriting and servicing small-dollar loans. Banks and credit unions have simply been unable to duplicate the traditional installment loan model in an economically unsuccessful way. The services' military aid societies have neither the mission nor the financial capacity to meet the financing needs of a large and diverse military population without a significant infusion of charitable donations or taxpayer subsidies. While the aid societies do provide critical assistance to servicemembers in challenging and difficult circumstances, often with nowhere else to turn, they simply are not designed to fulfill the role of serving normal small-dollar credit needs in the general marketplace. In fact, AFSA members report that many of their clients come to them specifically because their credit needs fall outside of the limited scope of the general lending guidelines of the military aid societies, which are designed to assist in emergencies and special circumstances.

---

[8] Department of Defense Report on Predatory Lending Practices Directed at Members of the Armed Forces and their Dependents. August 9, 2006.

[9] 32 *CFR* 232. Limitations on Terms of Consumer Credit Extended to Service Members and Dependents; Final Rule. August 31, 2007.

[10] Department of Defense Report on Implementation of Limitations on Terms of Consumer Credit Extended to Service Members and Dependents. July 22, 2008.

Installment Loans Help Meet the Unique Needs of Servicemembers and their Families

Small-dollar, traditional installment loans help meet the needs of servicemembers and their families. Some AFSA members lend money to servicemembers as they are getting ready to deploy. Servicemembers often must borrow in order to procure additional supplies they will need in the combat environment, such as body armor. They also borrow before they deploy in order to get their households in order and to have an amount of emergency cash on hand to be available to their spouses and families. An increase in debt consolidation loans is seen at this time as well.

Permanent change-of-station moves, overseas assignments, and relocations are some of the more prevalent reasons why servicemembers borrow. Often servicemembers say that there is never enough money available to move and that they need additional funds to supplement what the military provides. Physical moving costs, security deposits and new appliances are all expenses that are incurred during a move. AFSA members making these loans recognize this "purpose of loan" as bona fide and as such, are willing to extend small-dollar credit to meet these needs.

* * *

AFSA believes that it is important to ensure that access to beneficial forms of credit is preserved for members of the military community while, at the same time, ensuring that sensible consumer protections are maintained. We appreciate the Commerce Committee holding this hearing on aggressive business practices that some soldiers and their families face, as well as ways to protect servicemembers from abusive behavior. AFSA looks forward to continuing to work with Congress and Federal regulators to improve the quality of life for military families.

Please feel free to contact AFSA Executive Vice President Bill Himpler with any questions. *bhimpler@afsamail.org.*

The CHAIRMAN. So ordered.

STATEMENT OF HON. BILL NELSON, U.S. SENATOR FROM FLORIDA

Senator NELSON. Mr. Chairman, may I ask you a question?

Why in the world would the Department of Defense constrict the definition of consumer credit from the very broad consumer protection bill that we, with the Joint Chiefs of Staff urging us, passed in 2006?

The CHAIRMAN. I do not know the answer to that question, as I do not know the answer to—to me a rather shocking thing. I think in most parts in the Department of Defense, maybe not all of the services but most of them, that when soldiers and men and women leave the military—their time is up, they don't get a health checkup—they get no health checkup. So if the person has PTSD, it's going to be for somebody else to find out. If the person has mental health problems, it's going to be for somebody else to find. I can't answer your question and I can't answer my question.

It's a very, very good group and I thank you very, very much for coming. Let's start with the Honorable Robert Cooper, the Attorney General for the State of Tennessee.

STATEMENT OF HON. ROBERT E. COOPER, JR., ATTORNEY GENERAL, STATE OF TENNESSEE

Mr. COOPER. Thank you, Mr. Chairman.

Chairman Rockefeller, Ranking Member Thune, Committee members, it's an honor to be included with this distinguished panel today. And I congratulate the Committee Chair and this committee for taking on this important subject.

I want to use my limited time to talk about a case, as you alluded to, that we handled in the Tennessee Attorney General's Office against companies that were targeting soldiers in Tennessee with numerous unlawful business practices. And after I've done that, I want to touch on just a few lessons that we have learned from that litigation.

The lawsuit began in 2005 when the Tennessee Attorney General's Office filed a complaint in state court, obtained a temporary restraining order, an asset freeze, and other relief against Britlee Inc., a seller of computers and other electronics, and Rome Finance Company, which was financing these sales.

These companies were targeting active duty soldiers at Fort Campbell, which is on the Tennessee-Kentucky border north of Nashville. Our lawsuit alleged that Rome Finance and Britlee both engaged in numerous unlawful practices. And some of those included: First, operating without appropriate licenses in Tennessee, claiming their prices on computers and electronics were a great deal but instead price gouging soldiers by marking up their products by as much as 300 percent of the manufacturers recommended price; falsely representing that their products were new when, in fact, many were returns, liquidation purchases, and defective equipment; falsely claiming that they were offering zero percent financing, this was called at different times free financing, 100 percent military financing, special programs for servicemembers, but it was really a 19.2 percent APR not counting other hidden fees in contract terms that were in the arrangement; and then engaging in abusive collection practices, including contacting superior officers.

And when we filed the lawsuit, Rome Finance responded with an aggressive litigation strategy and engaged in extensive misconduct during discovery; refusing to produce documents, destroying records, and walking out on depositions. However, the most egregious example of abusive conduct by Rome during the litigation was that it continued for several months, despite notice from our office, to attempt collection on the account of a deceased soldier whose body was found on the streets of Baghdad after being tortured and beheaded. Responding to this, the state court judge observed in his decision, "While the thought of what these soldier's families had to endure when these soldiers were killed in action is unbearable, the thought that their families and loved ones had to endure months and months of unnecessary collection billings from Rome is beyond comprehension." And as an addendum to our written statement we have included the findings and conclusion of the court.

Now, three years after the complaint was filed, in August 2008, the court granted the ultimate sanction for Rome Finances's litigation misconduct, which is that it entered a default judgment against the company. At the hearing that day the state presented its case, submitted proof of the amount of restitution owed to the soldiers who had done business with these companies and the court ordered that restitution. It also ordered the companies to stop all collections against soldiers; dismissed all collections lawsuits; ordered Rome to clear up all affected credit bureau records for the soldiers; remaining debts were ordered canceled; and the soldiers were allowed to keep their computers.

I'd like to say that the case was over at that point, but it wasn't. Rome Finance then went to California where it was incorporated and file a Chapter 11 bankruptcy in an attempt to enjoin the state court proceedings. Fortunately, that failed and, while those bankruptcy proceedings are still underway, we negotiated with the trustee in the case to obtain approval for the disbursement of $2.2 million from Rome's assets. And that money has been used to provide restitution to almost 4,000 soldiers who bought merchandise from these companies. And I will say that, before the hearing from Ms. Nelson, these two companies are now doing business in New York and are the subject of investigation by that office.

Now let me talk about some of the lessons that we've learned from this litigation. First, many unscrupulous business that now prey on our military and their families no longer fit the profile of a local business on the strip outside the main gate. While Britlee did have a kiosk in the local mall, which was near Fort Campbell, Rome, Britlee and their strategic partners were sophisticated, nationwide operations with tens of millions of dollars in cash-flow. They had financial resource and expertise not only to hide their assets, but to close and reopen where opportunity called; such as in New York.

Second point deals with some of the obstacles that we ran into in prosecution. In our case, Rome Finance falsely claimed that it was a duly licensed consumer lender in California. It was not. When these companies failed to register, that puts an even greater burden on state regulators who have administrative procedures to deal with license entities, but then have to go to court to close down those who are operating outside the regulatory framework.

Another enforcement obstacle is the cost of proceeding against these national operations. Here, as I said, the company went to California to file bankruptcy to escape the Tennessee judgment. And as a result, our lawyers had to go to California several times. This was not cheap. Fortunately, we had the resources to pursue this, but it can be a real financial challenge for State Attorneys Generals to obtain judgments and then have to chase the defendant, not around the state to collect, but around the country.

Now, let me shift this discussion to the people we are trying protect, that is our service men and women. A number of factors, which the Committee has alluded to, make the soldiers at Fort Campbell and other bases vulnerable to sophisticated operators like Rome/Britlee. Many younger soldiers are simply less experienced and less sophisticated about financial matters. A large number of soldiers who purchased computers from Britlee were motivated purchasers about to be deployed and desperate to have some means to communicate back home. And then, once soldiers were locked into these abusive financial agreements, they were afraid that their consumer dispute would be viewed negatively by their commanders and would harm their advancement so they were hesitant to report or complain.

Now, another significant problem encountered by soldiers involved the use of allotments; automatic deductions from their paychecks. Rome/Britlee made effective use of this tool; had the soldiers making a purchase go online on the spot, access their military pay accounts, and setup pay accounts in Kentucky. Predictably, these payments were very difficult to stop even after the court enjoined further collection.

But if I wanted to point out one thing in the brief time I have left, is the importance of financial education of young soldiers and communication with young soldiers and their families. They need to understand not only how to manage, but to feel comfortable talking about their problems. We became involved in this case only because a number of soldiers complained to the Consumer Affairs Counselors at Fort Campbell who then brought it to our attention. If the counselors had not been doing their job, talking to soldiers and as well doing their job in talking to our office, this case may not have come to light. So that communication needs to go on, not only within the base but also between the base and state enforcement authorities like the Attorney General's Office.

During the litigation, we met and talked regularly at Fort Campbell, with the Commanding General, General McConville, down the chain of command to the civilian—consumer protection teams. And we are currently working with the Consumer Affairs counselors to develop training material on consumer protection issues tailored specifically to military bases.

So, that communication is extraordinarily important. That's one reason why it's so important to have Holly Petraeus leading the effort at CFPB to protect servicemembers. She and I have visited Fort Campbell together, other bases in Tennessee. She spoke earlier at a bipartisan conference of State Attorneys General in Nashville that dealt with issues facing military faces in the south. And I can personally attest to her unique ability to facilitate communication between military and civilian authorities.

So, training in financial literacy is important to all aspects of society, but it's particularly important to maintaining military force readiness and morale so that are men and women in uniform can focus on their mission and not worry about their financial condition. Fort Campbell is doing a good job, but we understand that the military can't assume the entire burden and that's why we need a strong partnership among the military, Federal agencies, state consumer offices, and State Attorneys General to protect our men and women in uniform from consumer fraud.

Thank you, Mr. Chairman.

[The prepared statement of Mr. Cooper follows:]

PREPARED STATEMENT OF ROBERT E. COOPER, JR., ATTORNEY GENERAL, STATE OF TENNESSEE

Good afternoon Chairman Rockefeller, Ranking Member John Thune and members of the Committee. It is an honor to be included on this distinguished panel and to testify before you today. I congratulate the Committee for its leadership on this important issue. I want to use my limited time to discuss a judgment obtained by the office of the Tennessee Attorney General against companies that were targeting soldiers at the Ft. Campbell army base with numerous unlawful practices. I will conclude with some lessons learned from this six-year legal battle.

The lawsuit began in 2005 when the Tennessee Attorney General's office obtained a Temporary Restraining Order (TRO), an asset freeze, and other relief against Britlee, Inc., a seller of computers and other electronics, and Rome Finance Company, which financed these sales.

Our lawsuit alleged that Rome Finance and Britlee both engaged in numerous unlawful practices including:

- operating without appropriate licenses in Tennessee;
- price-gouging soldiers;
- falsely representing their products were new when in fact many were returns, liquidation purchases, and defective equipment;
- claiming their prices on computers and electronics were a great deal, but marking up their products as high as 300 percent of MSRP;
- falsely claiming they were offering 0 percent financing, but really charging 19.2 percent APR;
- concealing additional costs and contract terms; and
- engaging in abusive collection practices, including contacting superior officers.

Rome Finance adopted an aggressive litigation strategy and engaged in misconduct during discovery. However, the most egregious example of abusive conduct by Rome was that it continued for seven months, despite notice from our office, to attempt collection on the account of a deceased soldier whose body was found on the streets of Baghdad after being tortured and beheaded. State Circuit Court Judge R. Ross Hicks observed in his decision, "While the thought of what these soldier's families had to endure when these soldiers were killed in action is unbearable, the thought that their families and loved ones had to endure months and months of unnecessary collection billings from Rome is beyond comprehension." [1]

On August 11, 2008, the court granted the ultimate sanction for Rome Finances's litigation misconduct—a default judgment. At a hearing that day, the State presented its case against Rome and submitted proof of the amount of restitution to which the soldiers were entitled. The court ordered the companies to stop all collections against soldiers, dismissed all collections lawsuits, and ordered Rome to clear up all affected credit bureau records for the soldiers. Remaining debts were ordered cancelled, and the soldiers were allowed to keep their computers.

Rome Finance then filed Chapter 11 bankruptcy in California in a failed attempt to enjoin the state court proceeding. Because of Rome's misconduct that had been documented in our case, a trustee was appointed in the bankruptcy proceeding with the support of the U.S. Department of Justice. Those bankruptcy proceedings are still under way, but my office was able to negotiate and obtain approval from the bankruptcy trustee for the disbursement of $2.2 million from Rome's assets, which has been used to provide restitution to almost 4,000 soldiers who had bought merchandise from these companies.

Unbeknownst to the State, after we obtained the TRO, Rome Finance and Britlee created a host of new entities to do additional business in other states, and Rome began transferring receivables to its new entities. We were subsequently contacted by the New York Attorney General's Watertown office in connection with its investigation of the new Rome and Britlee entities that were operating near a military base in New York.

This is the first lesson learned from the Rome/Britlee case. Many unscrupulous businesses that prey on our military and their families no longer fit the profile of the local business on "the strip" outside the main gate. In this case, Britlee set up kiosks in the local mall alongside reputable merchants. More important, the retailer and its strategic partners in finance were sophisticated, nationwide operations with tens of millions of dollars in cash flow. They had the financial resources and expertise not only to hide assets but to close and re-open where opportunity called.

Shifting operations around the country is easier when a company doesn't worry about obtaining proper licenses and lies about its licensing status when caught. For example, Rome Finance falsely claimed it was a duly licensed consumer lender in California. This practice puts an even greater burden on regulators, who have administrative procedures to deal with licensed entities but have to seek a court order to close down those operating outside the regulatory framework.

The defendants in our case engaged in an aggressive litigation strategy, including filing bankruptcy in California, to avoid paying the Tennessee court's substantial judgment. This tactic required our lawyers to make several trips to California. Fortunately, my office had the resources and staff time available for this case. Litigation against companies experienced in preying on the military is difficult and time-consuming. It can be a challenge for state Attorneys General who, although they

---

[1] *State of Tennessee ex rel. Robert E. Cooper, Jr., Attorney General* v. *Britlee, Inc., et al.*, Case No. 50500795,slip op. at 43 (Montgomery County Cir. Ct, Dec. 18, 2008 Findings of Fact and Conclusions of Law).

may win a judgment in state court, have limited resources available to chase defendants around the country.

Defendants in this and other cases who prey on our men and women in uniform will go to great lengths to stay in business because it is very lucrative. Discovery in our case revealed that the defendants were funded by a network of sophisticated investors attracted by high rates of return. Unfortunately, many young soldiers are less sophisticated about finance and are especially vulnerable. A large number of soldiers who purchased computers from Britlee were about to be deployed to Iraq and were desperate to have some means to communicate back home. Unscrupulous retailers and lenders know that soldiers will hesitate to report them to regulators and are afraid consumer disputes will be viewed negatively by their commanders and will harm their advancement.

Another problem encountered by soldiers in the Rome/Britlee case involved the use of allotments. An allotment is an automatic deduction made from a soldier's military-pay account which is sent to a third party. Allotments can be discretionary (where the soldiers instructs the military where to send some or all of his money) and non-discretionary (where the soldier's pay is allotted to someone else by mandate, such as court-ordered child support). This system of allotments through a third-party bank is commonly used by military predatory lenders because allotments made to "entities" must be made by electronic transfer or direct deposit and are difficult to stop once they have started.

In this case, Britlee required soldiers making a purchase at its mall kiosk to go online on the spot, access their military pay accounts (known My Pay accounts), and set up bank accounts at First Citizens Bank in Kentucky. The bank was designated to receive regular allotment payments from the soldiers' military pay, which the bank would then send to Rome Finance every month on behalf of the soldiers. Predictably, these payments were very difficult to stop even after the court enjoined further collections.

Perhaps the most important lesson learned from the Rome/Britlee lawsuit is the importance of financial education and communication with young soldiers and their families. The Attorney General's office became involved in this case at the request of the Consumer Affairs Counselors at Ft. Campbell after a number of soldiers complained to them about Rome/Britlee. During the litigation, our office communicated regularly with Ft. Campbell, from the Commander down the chain of command to the civilian consumer protection team. We meet regularly with Ft. Campbell's Consumer Affairs Counselors and are currently working with them to develop training materials on consumer protection issues tailored specifically to military bases.

There is no substitute for a close working relationship and communication between civilian and military authorities to protect our military from predatory and unfair practices. That is one reason it is so important to have Holly Petraeus leading the effort at the Consumer Financial Protection Bureau to protect servicemembers. Ms. Petraeus and I have visited Ft. Campbell and military facilities in Memphis together. She spoke earlier this year at a bipartisan conference my office hosted for the southern region of the National Association of Attorneys General on consumer and other legal issues facing the many military bases in the South. I can personally attest to her unique ability to facilitate communication between the military and civilian consumer protection authorities.

A 2009 investigation by this Committee highlighted unique challenges the Internet presents in the area of consumer protection. Young soldiers and their families, often living in places far away from friends and family, are prime targets for every kind of digital fraud, unfair business practice, and predatory lending. In the Rome/Britlee litigation, we had the advantage that our defendants could be sued and had assets within the United States. Unfortunately, bad actors using the Internet, especially those on servers from non-U.S. jurisdictions, can be impossible to stop. Even if you obtain a judgment, it is virtually impossible to enforce.

These difficulties in enforcement highlight the need for broader financial literacy education, so that consumers, both civilians and military, do not fall prey to these frauds. Tennessee is one of the few states that mandate financial literacy training for high school students. In fact, a member of my staff helps to lead the program that educates teachers around our state on this subject. More and more private sector employers are realizing that financial literacy is essential to a stable and efficient workforce. And financial literacy is just as important to maintaining military force readiness and morale, so that our servicemen and women can focus on their mission without the distraction of unnecessary financial issues. Ft. Campbell is doing a good job in this area, but we cannot expect the military to assume the entire burden. We need a strong partnership among the military, Federal agencies, state consumer offices, and state attorneys general to protect our men and women in uniform from consumer fraud.

Mr. CHAIRMAN. Thank you very, very much, General Cooper.

Ms. Holly Petraeus has been with us before. Everybody admires her for what she does. She's the Assistant Director of the Consumer Financial Protection Bureau for the Office of Servicemember Affairs. She's a hard charger. She knows what she is talking about. And I would not want to be on the wrong side of her ledger.

Please proceed.

STATEMENT OF HOLLISTER K. PETRAEUS, ASSISTANT DIRECTOR, CONSUMER FINANCIAL PROTECTION BUREAU, OFFICE OF SERVICEMEMBER AFFAIRS

Ms. PETRAEUS. Thank you, Chairman Rockefeller, Ranking Member Thune, and distinguished members of the Committee. I appreciate the opportunity to testify today.

For those of you who are not familiar with the Office of Servicemember Affairs, we are responsible for educating servicemembers and their families to make better informed financial decision; from monitoring complaints to the bureau; from servicemembers and their families; and for coordinating with other Federal and state agencies on consumer protection measures for the military.

Obviously, although we address many consumer protection issues, my mission ties in very directly to the issue of predatory lending to the military. And I've lived on or near military bases my entire life and seen that strip outside the gates, offering everything from furniture to used cars to electronics to jewelry and the high-cost credit to pay for them. But in the early 2000s, there was an alarming increase in the number of businesses offering payday loans, and a corresponding increase in the number of servicemembers taking advantage of that easy money, often without the ability to repay what they borrowed.

The Pentagon took note that indebtedness was beginning to take a serious toll on military readiness as did the media. And two academics undertook a major study in 2005, looking at the geographic distribution of payday lenders across the United States. Professors Chris Peterson and Steven Graves described "An environment where servicemembers are literally surrounded by lenders clamoring to charge annual rates averaging around 450 percent. Payday lenders crowd around the gates of military bases like bears on a trout stream."

In 2006, at the request of Congress, the Department of Defense published a report on predatory lending practices directed at members of the armed forces and their dependence. It found that "Predatory lending undermines military readiness, harms the morale of troops and their families, and adds to the cost of fielding in all volunteer fighting force."

Congress passed the bipartisan Talent-Nelson Amendment, also known as the Military Lending Act or MLA, and it was signed into law in 2006. And I should note with appreciation that one of the authors, Senator Bill Nelson, is on this committee and here today.

The MLA caps the rate on consumer credit to a covered member of the armed forces or a dependent of a covered member at 36 percent and creates other consumer protections as well. The Department of Defense was given the task of writing the regulations for the Military Lending Act and opted to define consumer credit as only three types of loans defined fairly narrowly. They are payday loans: closed-end loans with terms of 91 days or fewer for $2,000 or less; auto title loans: closed-end loans of terms of 181 days or fewer; and tax refunded participation loans, which are closed-end credit.

For those products that fall within the Department's definitions, the law has had a positive impact. But, the concern now is that lenders have easily found ways to get outside of the definitions.

In my almost three years at the Bureau I have been to more than 70 bases and National Guard units. Here are just a few of the stories I've hear: The spouse of a wounded warrior in the Illinois National Guard took out an auto title loan of $2,575 at an APR of 300 percent. The finance charges on the loan were over $5,000. The loan was not subject to the MLA because it was longer than 181 days.

Servicemembers from North Carolina and Delaware each took out loans at 584 percent. The loans were not subject to the Act's protections because they were open-end lines of credit.

At Joint Base McGuire-Dix-Lakehurst, in New Jersey, a sailor had one loan at 499 percent and another at 197 percent; neither covered by the MLA. He was paying over 66 percent of his take-home pay on those two loans.

Concerns about the effectiveness of the current rule have led to renewed interest from Congress. Recently, thanks in large part to the efforts of Senators Reed, Blumenthal and others; we have seen updates to the Act which provided enforcement authority for the Act of Federal regulators, including the Bureau.

And our efforts are already reaping dividends when it comes to enforcing the Act. Just this morning, the Bureau announced an enforcement action against a large national payday lender, Cash America, which had made loans in violation of the MLA to hundreds of servicemembers or their dependents. As part of the enforcement action, the lender refunded loan and loan-related fees for a total amount of approximately $33,550. It also put additional compliance mechanisms in place and agreed to increase training on the MLA for its customer service representatives.

This is a great example of what can be achieved through the combined efforts of the Bureau's supervisory and enforcement areas; a significant change in a large payday lenders appreciation of, in compliance with, the MLA. I still have real concerns; however, about the ability of lenders to easily evade the current MLA regulations. The original rule was effective for those products that it covered, but over the past 6 years we have seen significant changes in the type of products offered and the contours of state law. And I think it's critically important to ensure that the MLA protections keep up.

I believe that any approach that has strict definitions that define individual products will fall victim to the same evasive tactics that are plaguing the current rule. I also believe that, from a military financial readiness point of view, it makes no difference whether the loan is made by a depository institution or a non-depository institution, nor does it matter whether the loan is structured as open or closed-end. A loan with a sky-high interest rate and burdensome fees has the same adverse impact on military financial readiness no matter who offers it.

In sum, the underlying goals of protecting military and financial readiness, led to the passage of the MLA in 2006, are as important today as they were when the act was originally passed. And I think we should all be indignant when we hear our servicemembers trapped in outrageous loans and realize that there's little we can do under the current regulations because they are just longer than 91 days or structured as open-end credit. We owe it to our servicemembers and their families to do the best possible job of crafting the rules that properly implement the intent of the Military Lending Act.

I look forward to working with you, the department, and all stakeholders who have an interest in accomplishing these goals.

Thank you.

[The prepared statement of Ms. Petraeus follows:]

PREPARED STATEMENT OF HOLLISTER K. PETRAEUS, ASSISTANT DIRECTOR, CONSUMER FINANCIAL PROTECTION BUREAU, OFFICE OF SERVICEMEMBER AFFAIRS

Chairman Rockefeller, Ranking Member Thune, and distinguished Members of the Committee, I'd like to thank you for the opportunity to speak with you today concerning consumer protection for the military, particularly in the area of predatory lending to servicemembers and their families.

Many of you already know me as I've testified before you on other committees, and I've also had the opportunity to visit with some of you in your home States. But for those of you who are not familiar with my office, the Office of Servicemember Affairs at the Consumer Financial Protection Bureau (Bureau or CFPB), I'd like to take a few moments to tell you what we do.

As laid out in the Dodd-Frank Act, the Office of Servicemember Affairs at the Bureau is responsible for:

- Developing and implementing initiatives to educate and empower servicemembers and their families to make better-informed decisions regarding consumer financial products and services;
- Monitoring complaints submitted by servicemembers and their families about consumer financial products and services, and the responses to those complaints; and
- Coordinating the efforts of Federal and State agencies, as appropriate, regarding consumer protection measures relating to consumer financial products and services offered to, or used by, servicemembers and their families.

Obviously my mission ties in very directly to the issues that you'd like to address today. Before I go into what we're doing at the Bureau when it comes to predatory lending, however, I'd like to add a little historical perspective. Before I came to the Bureau, I was at the Council of Better Business Bureaus from 2004 to 2010, running their BBB Military Line program. In that role, I had a ringside seat for the fight to create and pass the original Military Lending Act (MLA), which was designed to protect servicemembers from the predatory lenders that were springing up around military bases in ever-increasing numbers.

I've lived on or near military installations my entire life, and it's a fact that a great many of them have a "strip" of businesses outside the gates, offering military families everything from furniture to used cars to electronics to jewelry—and the high-cost credit to pay for them, as well. But in the early 2000s there was an alarming increase in the number of businesses offering the new phenomenon of "payday loans," and a corresponding increase in the number of servicemembers taking advantage of that easy money, often without the ability to repay what they borrowed. To cite evidence from one of the military relief societies: "In 2001, Navy-Marine Corps Relief Society provided only $5,000 to 9 servicemembers falling victim to the predatory lending industry. In 2006, Navy-Marine Corps Relief Society provided over 1.37 million dollars to military members and/or families who were victimized by predatory lenders."[1]

The Pentagon took notice of the fact that indebtedness was beginning to take a serious toll on military readiness. On May 3, 2006, Adm. Mike Mullen, [then] Chief of Naval Operations wrote in an administrative memo to Navy personnel: "A sailor's financial readiness directly impacts unit readiness and the Navy's ability to accomplish its mission. . . . I am concerned with the number of sailors who are taken advantage of by predatory lending practices, the most common of which is the payday loan."[2] The national news media also took note: "Thousands of U.S. troops are being barred from overseas duty because they are so deep in debt they are considered security risks, according to an Associated Press review of military records."[3]

And two academics undertook a major study of the problem in 2005, looking at the geographic distribution of payday lenders across the U.S. to see if there was, in fact, a disproportionate number of payday lenders targeting military personnel.[4] Professors Chris Peterson and Steven Graves examined the density of payday lenders in 20 states. Their work described "an environment where servicemembers are literally surrounded by lenders clamoring to charge annual rates averaging around 450 percent."[5] They showed that even considering other variables such as income and ethnicity, the counties and zip codes that had the greatest overrepresentation of payday lenders tended to have one thing in common: proximity to large military populations. For example, in California, Texas, Virginia, and Washington (states with large servicemember populations), the study showed at least 60 percent of the 20 highest payday lending zip codes were associated with military installations. To quote Peterson and Graves: "payday lenders crowd around the gates of military bases like bears on a trout stream."[6]

By 2005, the use of high-cost credit targeting servicemembers was being discussed in the halls of Congress, and Senator Elizabeth Dole requested that the Department of Defense (Department or DOD) report on predatory lending practices. On August 9, 2006 the Department did just that, publishing a report entitled "Report On Predatory Lending Practices Directed at Members of the Armed Forces and Their Dependents." The report found that: "predatory lending undermines military readiness, harms the morale of troops and their families, and adds to the cost of fielding an all-volunteer fighting force. Education, counseling, assistance from Aid Societies, and sound alternatives are necessary but not sufficient to protect Service members from predatory lending practices or products that are aggressively marketed to consumers in general and to military personnel directly."[7]

Senator Dole stated at a Senate Banking hearing to discuss the report: "Predatory lenders are blatantly targeting our military personnel, undermining their financial stability and tarnishing their service records. This practice not only creates financial problems for individual soldiers and their families, but also weakens our military's operational readiness. . . ."[8]

Then-Undersecretary of Defense for Personnel and Readiness David Chu at that same hearing stated: "We need legislative action, to get to the bottom line because without it, we cannot curtail the migration of this set of predatory practice to other products."[9]

Congress passed the bipartisan Talent-Nelson Amendment (also known as the Military Lending Act) in 2006 and it was signed into law on October 17, 2006 (P.L. 109–364) (10 U.S.C. 987)—and I should note, with appreciation, that one of the authors, Senator Bill Nelson, is on this Committee. Senator Talent said of the amendment, "The fact is, predatory payday lenders are targeting American troops and are trying to make a buck off of their service to our country. We rely on the military to protect us, and we have just taken a significant step to protect them from predatory lenders."[10]

---

[1] *http://www.cnic.navy.mil/regions/ndw/installations/nsa_annapolis/ffr/support_services/counseling_and_assistance/personal_finance_management/danger_of_payday_loans.html*
[2] Navy League, Sea Power Magazine, June 2006
[3] *http://www.nbcnews.com/id/15337932/ns/us_news-military/t/debt-holds-us-troops-back-overseas-duty/#.UlLD3tKkrYc*
[4] Steven M. Graves & Christopher L. Peterson, Predatory Lending and the Military: The Law and Geography of "Payday" Loans in Military Towns, 66 OHIO ST. L.J. 653, 672 (2005) *http://www.law.fsu.edu/faculty/2005workshops/peterson.pdf*
[5] Graves & Peterson, p. 153.
[6] Graves & Peterson, p. 145.
[7] *http://www.defense.gov/pubs/pdfs/Report_to_Congress_final.pdf*
[8] *http://www.gpo.gov/fdsys/pkg/CHRG-109shrg50303/html/CHRG-109shrg50303.htm*
[9] *Ibid.*
[10] *http://www.gpo.gov/fdsys/pkg/CREC-2006-06-22/pdf/CREC-2006-06-22-pt1-PgS6406.pdf*

The Talent-Nelson Amendment does two important things for military consumers: (1) it expressly caps the rate at which a creditor extends consumer credit to a covered member of the armed forces or a dependent of a covered member, prohibiting annual percentage rates, including fees, greater than thirty-six percent; and (2) it creates a series of consumer protections for covered members and dependents (for example, a prohibition on the mandatory use of an allotment to repay the debt and a prohibition on requiring a covered member or dependent to submit to arbitration to resolve disputes related to the credit contract).

DOD was given the task of drafting implementing regulations (32 C.F.R. Part 232) for the Military Lending Act, and they were published on August 31, 2007. DOD opted to define consumer credit covered by the Act to include only three types of consumer loans, and to define those fairly narrowly. In general, the three types of loans are:

- Payday loans: closed-end loans with terms of 91 days or fewer, for $2,000 or less;
- Auto title loans: closed-end loans with terms of 181 days or fewer; and
- Refund anticipation loans: closed-end credit.

I think it is widely accepted that for those products that fall within the Department's definition of "consumer credit" the law has had a positive impact. When the Consumer Federation of America took a look at the Military Lending Act five years after implementation, they concluded: "To the extent products met these definitions, the law has been largely effective in curbing predatory payday, car title, and tax refund lending to covered borrowers."[11] However, the MLA's protections only apply if the credit product falls within the DOD's limited definition of consumer credit. For example, even if a servicemember or their spouse takes out a payday loan with a military annual percentage rate (MAPR) in excess of 36 percent, agencies with administrative enforcement authority under the law are unable to enforce the protections of the MLA if that loan is for a term greater than 91 days, over $2,000, or structured as open-end credit.

The increasing concern now is that lenders have easily found ways to get outside of the definitions in the current DOD rule implementing the MLA. As I testified before the Senate Banking Committee in June 2012: "I hear from financial counselors on the installations about the prevalence of payday-like products that are specifically marketed to military families—often with patriotic-sounding names and the American flags on the website to match, but with a sky-high interest rate for the servicemember who takes out the loan. And the Internet is full of 'military loans,' some outright scams and others with very high interest rates. Although the Military Lending Act put a 36 percent cap on the annual percentage rate of certain types of loans to the active-duty military, some lenders have found ways to get outside of the definitions in the Department of Defense (DOD) rule implementing the Military Lending Act."[12]

In some states, state law allows a broad range of high-cost credit products that fall outside of the narrow band of products covered by the current rule. For example, California, Texas, and Virginia—together home to more than a third of our active-duty servicemembers—all permit auto title loans of longer than 181days as well as high-cost installment loans. And in many states across the country, banks offer deposit-advance loans—lines of credit offered in connection with a borrower's deposit account. As discussed in more detail in the Bureau's recent white paper on payday loans and deposit advance products, when the Bureau used a special fee-based APR calculation in order to help compare deposit advance products to payday loans for purposes of the paper, it found that that APR could exceed 300 percent.

In my almost three years at the Bureau I have had the opportunity to visit more than 70 bases and National Guard Units. And at nearly every stop issues related to high-cost lending come up. Here are just a few of the stories I've heard on the road:

- The spouse of a wounded warrior in the Illinois National Guard took out an auto title loan of $2,575 at an APR of 300 percent. The finance charges on the loan were $5,720.24 for a total amount of $8,295.24. The loan was not subject to the Act's protections under the current rule because it had a term longer than 181 days.

---

[11] *http://www.consumerfed.org/pdfs/Studies.MilitaryLendingAct.5.29.12.pdf*
[12] *http://www.consumerfinance.gov/newsroom/written-testimony-of-holly-petraeus-before-the-senate-committee-on-banking-housing-and-urban-affairs/*

- At the Airman and Family Readiness Center at Travis Air Force Base, California I heard about a servicemember who borrowed $6,000. He financed this amount for 36 months at 102.47 percent APR. The loan cost the servicemember $13,463.04 and was secured by the title of his car. The loan was not subject to the MLA's protections under the current rule because it was for a term longer than 181 days.
- From one of the military aid societies I heard about servicemembers from North Carolina and Delaware who each took out loans at an APR of 584.68 percent. The loans were not subject to the Act's protections under the current rule because they were structured as open-end lines of credit.
- A JAG at Marine Corps Recruit Depot-San Diego had a client who took out an auto title loan of $10,000. The terms of the loan were 36 months with an APR of 101.9 percent. The Marine used his military ID to get the loan, so they were aware of his military status, but because the amount and duration of the loan exceeded the parameters of loans covered by the current rule the protections of the Act did not apply.
- A community readiness consultant at Joint Base McGuire-Dix-Lakehurst in New Jersey told me about a sailor with severe debt problems. He had one loan from a military-specific lender with an APR at 499 percent. This loan was not subject to the protections of the Military Lending Act because it was structured as an open-end line of credit. The sailor had a second loan at an APR of 197 percent with a balance of over $1,500. This loan was not subject to the Act's protections under the current rule because it was for a term longer than 91 days. The sailor was paying over 66 percent of his take-home pay trying to pay off these two loans.

There are also studies that have been done about the continued prevalence of high-cost lenders targeting military families. As part of its latest research on payday lending, The Pew Charitable Trusts found that: "5.9 percent of payday and auto title loan borrowers live in a household that includes current members of the Armed Services. Comparatively, 2.5 percent of U.S. households overall are active duty, in the National Guard, or in training. This difference is statistically significant."[13]

And DOD has also reported that: "(U)nscrupulous lenders have sought, and are seeking, to create products and services which fall outside of the MLA and the enforcement actions mentioned above. Several years removed from its enactment, however, our financial counselors and legal assistance attorneys still see clients who have payday or vehicle title loans. They also report that Internet and overseas opportunities exist to evade the law, and that some unscrupulous lenders—and even borrowers—still attempt to skirt or evade the law, by entering into loans that charge interest greater than 36 percent and contain terms that have been modified to avoid falling under the MLA. Creditors and lenders still attempt to avoid the MLA by utilizing procedures or modifying products to fall outside of the regulation."[14]

Concerns about the effectiveness of the current rule have led to renewed interest from Congress. Recently, thanks in large part to the efforts of Senators Reed, Blumenthal, and others, we have seen updates to the Act through amendments signed into law in January of this year. Based on those amendments, DOD is taking another look at the effectiveness of the MLA, which may include rewriting the rule as appropriate. And they provided enforcement authority for the Act to Federal regulators, including the Bureau. As a result, in September the Bureau announced amendments to our Supervision and Examination Manual incorporating the requirements of the Military Lending Act so our Supervision teams can be actively checking for compliance with the Act. We also released guidelines to our examiners on how to identify consumer harm and risks related to Military Lending Act violations when supervising payday lenders.[15]

I am happy to report that the Bureau's efforts are already reaping dividends when it comes to enforcing the protections of the Act. The Bureau announced just this morning an enforcement action against a large national payday lender which had made loans in violation of the MLA to hundreds of servicemembers or their dependents.

---

[13] Letter from Nick Bourke, Project Director, the Pew Charitable Trusts to Holly Petraeus, February 26, 2013.

[14] http://www.veterans.senate.gov/hearings.cfm?action=release.display&release_id=f3ab7d1a-7bbe-48ee-a476-9b812241ea8c

[15] http://www.consumerfinance.gov/newsroom/cfpb-lays-out-guidelines-for-protecting-servicemembers-in-the-payday-lending-market/

The examination of this lender uncovered that the company's large online payday lending subsidiary had mistakenly disabled its DOD database check during a software update in 2011—contributing to it having made 335 loans to active-duty military or dependents in violation of the MLA's Military Annual Percentage Rate (MAPR) provisions. The Bureau's examination also found that the company had made another 27 loans to protected military applicants during an 18-month period because the DOD eligibility check came back positive after the loan was already funded.

As part of the enforcement action, the lender refunded loan and loan-related fees on all identified loans, for a total amount of approximately $33,550. It also put additional compliance mechanisms in place and agreed to increased training on the MLA for its customer-service representatives. This is a great example of what can be achieved through the combined efforts of the Bureau's supervisory and enforcement areas: a significant change in a large payday lender's appreciation of, and compliance with, the MLA.

DOD has now begun exploring potential revisions to its existing regulation. It put an Advance Notice of Proposed Rulemaking (ANPR) in the *Federal Register* on June 17, 2013, requesting input from counselors, legal assistance attorneys, servicemembers, consumer protection advocacy groups, representatives of the financial services industry, and other interested parties.

The comments submitted in response detailed many of the concerns about evasion of the provisions of the MLA:

- The Colorado Attorney General wrote: "Given the narrow definitions, lenders have easily circumvented the purpose and protections intended by [the] MLA by simply offering 92 day loans, loans for $2001, or by structuring the loans as open-end credit."[16]

- Separately, a bipartisan group of 13 Attorneys General wrote: "While the MLA has been largely successful in curbing abusive lending in those categories covered by the Department's current rules, the narrow categories and definitions create large loopholes that permit lenders to fashion abusive or predatory transactions that avoid the MLA's protections."[17]

- Consumer advocates in Texas wrote: "Store visits conducted by Texas Appleseed in Killeen, Texas reveal that some storefronts surrounding military bases have pivoted to offering high-cost multiple-payment products to servicemembers. For example, at least one national payday lender with two locations in Killeen, both within three miles of Fort Hood, offers six-month multiple-payment payday loans up to $3000 with a fee of $22 for every $100 borrowed. Combined with $36.26 in interest and fees, a $1500 multiple-payment loan therefore costs the borrower $386.26 if the loan is paid back on schedule for an annual percentage rate of 581.72 percent. The MLA does not include these multiple-payment payday loans, even though they contribute to the cycle of debt."[18]

- Comments from the head of the Illinois Department of Veteran Affairs extended beyond the active-duty population: "Approximately one out of every ten veterans reported having more than $40,000 in unsecured debt. For many veterans, some of this debt is acquired while on active-duty, often from high-cost lenders that frequently target military bases." She also noted that in Illinois, "the current Department of Defense rule does not apply to all forms of payday lending permitted by state law. . . ."[19]

- 23 of your Senate colleagues also weighed in: "Due to the narrow definition of consumer credit, certain lenders are offering predatory loan products to servicemembers at exorbitant triple-digit effective interest rates and loan products that do not include the additional protections envisioned by the law. As such, a wide range of credit that is structured as open-ended versus closed-ended or that otherwise is structured to evade the limitations set forth in the current regulations fall completely outside the law's intended prohibitions."[20]

The Department has since asked a group of Federal agencies, including the Bureau, the Department of the Treasury, the Federal Deposit Insurance Corporation, the Federal Reserve Board of Governors, the Office of the Comptroller of the Cur-

---

[16] http://www.regulations.gov/#!documentDetail;D=DOD-2013-OS-0133-0034
[17] http://www.regulations.gov/#!documentDetail;D=DOD-2013-OS-0133-0002
[18] http://www.regulations.gov/#!documentDetail;D=DOD-2013-OS-0133-0016 (accessed July 31, 2013)
[19] http://www.regulations.gov/#!documentDetail;D=DOD-2013-OS-0133-0006 (internal citation omitted)
[20] http://www.regulations.gov/#!documentDetail;D=DOD-2013-OS-0133-0036

rency, the National Credit Union Administration, and the Federal Trade Commission, to assist it as it takes a fresh look at the MLA rule. In July of this year, Col. Paul Kantwill, Director of Legal Policy, Office of the Undersecretary for Personnel and Readiness, Department of Defense, testified before the Senate Veteran Affairs Committee: "the Department has assembled the Prudential Regulatory Agencies and the CFPB to explore revisions to the regulation. We have established a team of skilled economists and analysts to assist us in this initial rulemaking, in addition to a similarly-skilled team of drafters."[21] We are pleased to be helping the Department as they undertake this effort, and fully support the efforts of the Department and the working group.

Some parties have raised concerns about changes to the MLA regulations severely limiting access to credit for servicemembers. In fact, servicemembers do have lower-cost, less risky alternatives that are available to them, and that DOD encourages them to utilize.

For one thing, each branch of the service is supported by what is called a military relief society[22], which offers small no-interest loans and grants to servicemembers in need of emergency funds. In 2012, the relief societies provided $142.2 million in no-cost loans and grants to 159,745 clients.

As the Department noted however back in 2006: "We are continuing to improve the already substantial system of support available to them, but we need your assistance in limiting the availability of loans that fail to consider the ability of the borrower to repay so that servicemembers can and will consider other alternatives."[23]

In December of 2011, my office held a full-day Financial Fitness forum where one of the panels specifically discussed alternatives to high-cost, high-risk loan products.[24] Many of the programs that were highlighted at that forum were discussed as part of the Department's original report to Congress in 2006—where the DOD listed 24 different alternatives to high-cost loans.[25]

The bottom line, from my perspective based on what I have seen and heard in recent years, is that I have real concerns about the ability of lenders to easily evade the current MLA regulations. The original rule was effective for those products that it covered, but over the past 6 years we have seen significant changes in the type of products offered and the contours of state law, and I think it's critically important to ensure that the MLA protections keep up. I believe that any approach that has strict definitions that define individual products will fall victim to the same evasive tactics that are plaguing the current rule. And I know this is a shared concern with the Department.

I also believe that from a military financial readiness point of view it makes no difference whether the loan is made by a depository institution or a non-depository institution, nor does it matter whether the loan is structured as open-or closed-end. A loan with a sky-high interest rate, onerous arbitration requirements, and burdensome fees has the same adverse impact on military financial readiness no matter who offers it.

Also, as Senator Talent said back in 2006: "Our troops deserve uniform, national protection against abusive financial practices that target them." I do not see the logic in a soldier at Fort Drum, New York having different protections from one at Fort Hood, Texas.

I've heard quite frequently that DOD should fall back on financial education or command influence to deal with these issues. In fact, that was in some of the responses to the ANPR. On that subject I agree with what the Department wrote in the original preamble to the regulation:

> "It is not sufficient for the Department to train Service members on how best to use their financial resources. Financial protections are an important part of fulfilling the Department's compact with Service members and their families."[26]

In sum, the underlying goals of protecting military and financial readiness that led to passage of the MLA in 2006 are as important today as they were when the Act was originally passed. I think we should all be indignant when we hear of servicemembers trapped in outrageous loans and realize that there is little we can

---

[21] http://www.veterans.senate.gov/hearings.cfm?action=release.display&release_id=f3ab7d1a-7bbe-48ee-a476-9b812241ea8c
[22] Army Emergency Relief, Navy-Marine Corps Relief Society, Air Force Aid Society, Coast Guard Mutual Assistance
[23] http://www.gpo.gov/fdsys/pkg/CHRG-109shrg50303/html/CHRG-109shrg50303.htm
[24] http://files.consumerfinance.gov/f/201209_cfpb_Financial-Fitness-Whitepaper.pdf
[25] http://www.defense.gov/pubs/pdfs/Report_to_Congress_final.pdf
[26] http://www.gpo.gov/fdsys/pkg/FR-2007-08-31/pdf/07-4264.pdf

do under the current regulations because they are just longer than 91 days or structured as open-end credit. We owe it to our servicemembers and their families to do the best possible job of crafting rules that properly implement the intent of the Military Lending Act.

I'll close with a quote from Senator Elizabeth Dole who was a leader in getting the original Act passed: "Supporting our servicemembers means more than providing the equipment and training necessary for fighting. . . . We should also support their livelihood and their families, and predatory lending can seriously harm both."[27] I look forward to working with you, the Department and all stakeholders who have an interest in accomplishing these goals.

Thank you.

The CHAIRMAN. Thank you very much, Ms. Petraeus.

Mr. Charles Harwood, I have down Charles and I have down Chuck.

STATEMENT OF CHARLES HARWOOD, DEPUTY DIRECTOR, FEDERAL TRADE COMMISSION'S BUREAU OF CONSUMER PROTECTION

Mr. HARWOOD. Chuck.

The CHAIRMAN. Chuck, OK.

Mr. HARWOOD. Chuck, please. Thank you.

The CHAIRMAN. Mr. Chuck Harwood is Deputy Director of the Federal Trade Commission's Bureau of Consumer Protection, which is——

You have about 1,000 people working?

Mr. HARWOOD. I wish.

The CHAIRMAN. No. No. I don't mean you personally but——

[Laughter.]

Mr. HARWOOD. The Bureau of Consumer Protection is about 400–500 people; somewhere in that range.

The CHAIRMAN. OK.

Mr. HARWOOD. Yes.

The CHAIRMAN. All right.

Mr. HARWOOD. A thousand would be good though.

The CHAIRMAN. Yes.

Mr. HARWOOD. Yes.

The CHAIRMAN. You love sequester, don't you?

Mr. HARWOOD. Yes.

[Laughter.]

The CHAIRMAN. Please proceed.

Mr. HARWOOD. Thank you.

Chairman Rockefeller, Ranking Member Thune, and distinguished members of the Committee, thank you for the opportunity to describe the FTC's consumer protection efforts on behalf of servicemembers and their families. The Commission's official views are in the written statement that's been submitted to the Committee. My oral statement and answers to any questions are my views.

The FTC is dedicated to protecting servicemembers, veterans, and their families from fraudulent deceptive practices. This summer, for example, the Commission brought a case against one of the Nation's largest veterans home loan refinancers. The defendant, Morgan Investors Corporation, allegedly misrepresented cost and potential savings or free financing services offered to veterans,

---

[27] http://www.gpo.gov/fdsys/pkg/CHRG-109shrg50303/html/CHRG-109shrg50303.htm

continued to call military consumers in violation of Do Not Call, and falsely implied that loans were from the VA.

Notably, this is the commission's first action enforcing the Mortgage Acts and Practices-Advertising rule which, I believe, members of this committee helped us with. And they violated the rule by— we alleged by falsely representing that low-interest fixed-rate mortgages were available at no cost and by misrepresenting government affiliation.

The FTC obtained a sizable $7.5 million civil penalty as well as strong injunctive relief to remedy the violations.

In addition to deceptive schemes targeting military consumers, perpetrators of scams directed at the general population have been known to tailor their representations to the unique circumstances of military consumers. For example, in *FTC* v. *Goldman Schwartz,* the Commission presented evidence that a defendant debt collector used military related threats when attempting to collect from military consumers. One military consumer reported that the collector identified him as "a military liaison," and threatened to disclose the purported debt to the consumer's commander, told the consumer that indebtedness is grounds for dismissal from the military, and that the collector would ruin the consumer's military career.

An important resource in law enforcement actions like these is the FTC's Consumer Sentinel Complaint Network; it's a secure online database of more than 8 million consumer complaints. In 2002, the FTC and DOD jointly created military Sentinel, a sub part of consumer Sentinel. Among other things, Military Sentinel centralized the online collection of fraud complaints from the DOD and military communities.

Data from Consumer Sentinel and Military Sentinel shows that the top financial services complaint categories military consumers are debt collection, unlawful banking or lending practices, and scams offering mortgage foreclosure relief or debt management services. Now, these complaint categories are also FTC law enforcement priorities.

Since 2008, the FTC has filed 42 foreclosure relief cases, 34 debt relief cases, 20 payday lending cases, and 22 debt collection cases. Complimenting these consumer protection law enforcement efforts is the Commission's robust consumer education program. On its webpage, For Military Families, the Commission has assembled FTC materials that address the consumer challenges faced by servicemembers, veterans, and their families. For example, visitors to the page will find new FTC guidance about selecting a college particularly when using post-9/11 GI benefits. Visitors will also find, among other things, information about payday loans, credit reports, active duty alerts and deceptive schemes associated with veteran's pensions.

To expand the reach of our education efforts, the Commission relies on strong partnerships, such as the initiative we launched this year. On July 17, at events around the country, the FTC and others including DOD, Military Saves, and my colleagues at the CFPB, posted the first Military Consumer Protection Day to increase awareness of consumer protection issues that affects servicemembers, military families, veterans and even civilians in the military community.

Participating agencies and organizations further promoted the many free resources that are the first line of defense against fraud and it helped consumers make better informed money management decisions. We're already planning for our Military Consumer Protection Day 2014 and we know we'll be even bigger and better than last one.

Finally, the FTC also coordinates with its partners on military consumer protection policy initiatives. For example, through an interagency group, the commission is coordinating with DOD, CFPB, and others on possible amendments to DOD's military lending rule which we've already discussed. The recently amended Act also gives the FTC enforcement authority regarding refund anticipation payday and auto title loans.

The Commission—and I should add its staff as well—is grateful for the sacrifices that servicemembers and their families make and all of us are dedicated to providing them with pure-less consumer protection services.

Thank you very much.

[The prepared statement of Mr. Harwood follows:]

PREPARED STATEMENT OF THE FEDERAL TRADE COMMISSION, DELIVERED BY CHARLES A. HARWOOD, DEPUTY DIRECTOR, BUREAU OF CONSUMER PROTECTION, FEDERAL TRADE COMMISSION

Introduction

Chairman Rockefeller, Ranking Member Thune, and distinguished members of the Committee, I am Charles A. Harwood, Deputy Director of the Bureau of Consumer Protection of the Federal Trade Commission ("Commission" or "FTC").[1] I appreciate the opportunity to present the Commission's testimony on consumer protection issues impacting servicemembers and their families and the Commission's work in this area.

All consumers, including servicemembers, are potential targets for fraudsters, and combating fraud is a critical component of the Commission's consumer protection mission. That said, certain scams are more likely to target the military community, in part because military families may relocate frequently and many servicemembers—for the first time—are living on their own and earning a paycheck. Moreover, frauds against military consumers can undermine military readiness and troop morale. Accordingly, the Commission's efforts to eliminate such scams through aggressive enforcement and a vigorous, ongoing educational campaign are an important part of our consumer protection work.

This testimony outlines the areas of fraud that are most likely to affect the military community, describes our general enforcement in these areas, and lists some of the FTC's military-specific consumer education and outreach efforts.

II. Fraud Threats to Military Consumers

The FTC's consumer protection initiatives include combatting fraud in various areas that affect servicemembers, veterans, and their families. For example, just this summer, the Commission brought a case alleging that one of the Nation's largest refinancers of veterans' home loans made misleading claims directed at current and former servicemembers.[2] In the case, which was the first action to enforce the Mortgage Acts and Practices—Advertising Rule (MAP Rule), the Commission alleged the company violated by falsely representing that low interest, fixed-rate mortgages were available at no cost.[3] The Commission also alleged that the com-

---

[1] This written statement presents the views of the Federal Trade Commission. Oral statements and responses to questions reflect the views of the speaker and do not necessarily reflect the views of the Commission or any Commissioner.

[2] *United States* v. *Mortgage Investors Corp. of Ohio, Inc.*, No. 8:13–cv–01647–SDM–TGW (M.D. Fla. June 25, 2013), available at *http://www.ftc.gov/os/caselist/1223084/index.shtm.*

[3] The MAP Rule was promulgated by the FTC and recodified by the Consumer Financial Protection Bureau as Mortgage Acts and Practices—Advertising (Regulation N). *See* Mortgage Acts and Practices—Advertising Rule, 16 C.F.R. Part 321, recodified as Mortgage Acts and Prac-
Continued

pany violated the Do Not Call provisions of the Commission's Telemarketing Sales Rule. To resolve the allegations, the company agreed to pay a $7.5 million civil penalty, the largest fine the Commission has ever obtained in a case alleging Do Not Call violations.

Enforcement actions like these often flow from the Commission's active monitoring of the marketplace, which allows us to understand, identify, and ultimately eliminate threats to both military consumers and the public at large. As part of this monitoring, the Commission relies on the complaints we collect directly from consumers, our law enforcement experience, and collaborative initiatives with law enforcement partners, consumer groups, industry, academics, and others.

One of our most powerful tools in obtaining information about frauds is the FTC's Consumer Sentinel Complaint Network, a secure online database of more than 8 million consumer complaints available only to law enforcement. The database includes complaints that are reported directly to the FTC as well as to dozens of state law enforcement organizations, other Federal agencies, and non-governmental organizations such as the Better Business Bureau. These complaints act as an invaluable investigative tool for the thousands of federal, state, and local law enforcement agencies that have registered as members of Consumer Sentinel.

To ensure that servicemembers and their families can easily file consumer protection complaints with the FTC, in 2002 the FTC and the Department of Defense (DOD) jointly created Military Sentinel, a subset of Consumer Sentinel. Military Sentinel centralized the online collection of fraud complaints from the DOD and military communities. It also allows complaints to be recorded by branch of service and installation, giving government agencies—including DOD law enforcers and policymakers—vital information to better protect servicemembers and military civilians.[4]

The Commission is also working with the Departments of Veterans Affairs, Defense, Education, and Justice, and the Consumer Financial Protection Bureau (CFPB) to collect, through an online complaint system, feedback on problems with educational institutions experienced by the military community.[5] Veterans, servicemembers, and their families pursuing higher education through the Post-9/11 GI Bill and other education benefits can provide feedback on their schools through *gibill.va.gov/feedback*. When feedback is received, agencies will contact the school on behalf of the student and request a response within 90 days, and the complaints will be forwarded to Consumer Sentinel.

Data from Consumer Sentinel shows that the FTC received more than 42,200 fraud complaints from the military community out of the more than 1 million fraud complaints received in calendar year 2012.[6] The top complaint categories for military consumers were: debt collection; imposter scams;[7] fraud involving offers of prizes, sweepstakes, or gifts; unlawful banking or lending practices; and scams that offer mortgage foreclosure relief or debt management services.[8]

---

tices—Advertising (Regulation N), 12 C.F.R. Part 1014. The *Mortgage Investors* complaint included alleged violations of the MAP Rule and Regulation N.

[4] In 2011, the FTC's main Consumer Sentinel website was revamped to ensure that visitors to this complaint portal can provide the same military-specific demographic information. As a result, the Military Sentinel portals for different parts of the U.S. Armed Forces now direct visitors to the main Consumer Sentinel website.

[5] This initiative was launched pursuant to Executive Order 13607 (Apr. 27, 2012), available at *http://www.gpo.gov/fdsys/pkg/FR-2012-05-02/pdf/2012-10715.pdf*. The order addresses reports of misleading or predatory behavior towards military consumers and their families.

[6] These figures exclude Do Not Call registry and identity theft complaints.

[7] These involve scams in which the perpetrators pose as a friend, family member, or romantic interest, or claim an affiliation with a company or government agency, in order to induce people to send money or divulge personal information.

[8] Complaint data for 2013 shows similar patterns. From January 1, 2013 to September 30, 2013, we received approximately 33,923 fraud complaints from military consumers. Top complaint categories included: imposter scams (9,209); debt collection (4,174); banks and lenders (3,194); and prizes/sweepstakes/lotteries (2,225).

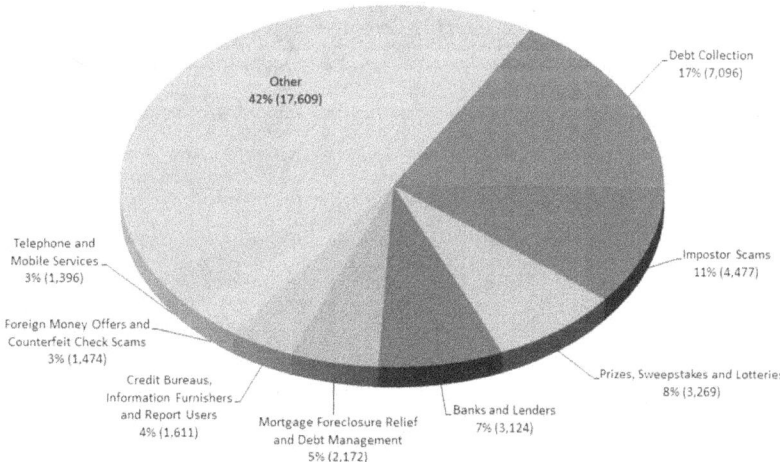

Top Complaint Categories for Military Consumers in Consumer Sentinel Network Complaints[1]
January 1 – December 31, 2012

[1] Percentages are based on the 42,228 military consumer complaints. These figures exclude Do Not Call registry and identity theft complaints.

Note: The section of the chart labeled "Other" represents complaints regarding over 100 other types of products, such as credit cards, unsolicited emails, advance-fee loans and credit arrangers, and spyware/adware/malware.

Source: Consumer Sentinel Network.

Notably, these complaint trends largely mirror those of the general population and include some of the FTC's highest consumer protection priorities—which we further describe below.[9]

In particular, many of these categories touch on the FTC's aggressive work to stop frauds related to consumer financial products and services, which has been one of the FTC's top priorities—particularly in the wake of the economic downturn. Since 2008, the FTC has been especially active in halting frauds targeting financially distressed consumers. We have brought:

- 42 cases and obtained monetary judgments totaling more than $190 million in the mortgage foreclosure relief area;
- 34 cases and obtained more than $300 million in judgments in debt relief matters;
- 20 cases and obtained over $120 million in monetary judgments protecting payday loan borrowers victimized by deceptive or unfair practices; and
- 22 cases and obtained more than $165 million in debt collection monetary judgments.[10]

In addition, the FTC has continued its efforts to eliminate fraud in the other areas raised in the complaints. For instance, since 2009, the FTC brought 22 law enforcement actions targeting purveyors of fraudulent business opportunity, work at home, and job scams, and filed 8 actions against scams offering prizes or sweepstakes.

The FTC's enforcement work has protected hundreds of thousands of consumers from unlawful practices, including members of the military community. In some instances, the FTC takes action against scammers that target the general population but tailor their practices to deceive military consumers. For example, in *FTC* v. *Goldman Schwartz,* the Commission presented evidence that a defendant debt collector that allegedly used a series of unlawful tactics in attempting to collect debts from consumers, used military-specific threats when attempting to collect from mili-

---

[9] One exception to this comparison is mortgage foreclosure relief and debt management services. This was the sixth highest complaint category for military members, in contrast to the fifteenth highest for the population as a whole.

[10] The monetary judgment amounts listed in this testimony include judgments that were suspended based on defendants' ability to pay.

tary consumers.[11] One military consumer reported that the collector identified itself as a "military liaison," threatened to disclose a purported debt to the consumer's commander, and told the consumer that indebtedness is grounds for dismissal from the military and that the collector would ruin the consumer's military career. Similarly, in *FTC v. NHS Systems, Inc.*, the Commission presented evidence that fraudulent telemarketers that preyed on the general public obtained some military consumers' financial information by falsely claiming to be calling from the IRS to offer special tax rebate checks to servicemembers.[12]

The FTC also targets frauds that specifically focus on servicemembers, veterans, and their families. As noted above, earlier this year the FTC filed a case against one of the Nation's leading refinancers of veteran's home loans, which led to a settlement in which the refinancer agreed to pay a $7.5 million civil penalty.[13] In offering refinancing services to current and former military consumers, the defendants allegedly: misrepresented the costs and potential savings of the services; continued to call military consumers, even after the consumers had informed the defendants that they did not wish to receive further calls or that their telephone numbers were listed with the National Do Not Call Registry; and implied that the loans they offered would come from Veterans Affairs or another government source. Along with the $7.5 million civil penalty, as part of the settlement the defendants agreed to an order imposing strong injunctive relief.

Additionally, the FTC's enforcement work extends to scams that target military families indirectly, including scams that prey on consumers that want to assist the U.S. Armed Forces community. For instance, as part of a coordinated federal-state crackdown on fraudulent telemarketers, the FTC brought an end to an allegedly sham non-profit that falsely claimed to provide financial assistance to the families of American soldiers fighting overseas. The Commission alleged that the defendants falsely claimed that donations would be used to provide care packages to veterans in VA hospitals and to support veteran's memorials.[14] As part of a settlement to resolve the FTC's allegations, the defendants agreed to a monetary judgment of more than $13 million and an order prohibiting future deceptive conduct.[15]

Finally, the Commission's enforcement work addresses practices of importance to the military community. For example, buying a car can be one of the most expensive and complicated financial transactions a military consumer will make. Since 2011, the FTC has brought 11 auto-related actions, involving a variety of unlawful conduct.[16] Many of these cases targeted practices that were identified in a series of three public roundtables that the Commission held on consumers' experiences when buying, financing and leasing motor vehicles.[17] Some of the roundtable panels specifically addressed practices that target military consumers, including various sales pitches geared to servicemembers and made on or near military bases, or on the Internet.[18] As part of the roundtables, the Commission also invited (and received) public comment on how these and other practices may impact members of the military.[19]

III. Military Consumer Education and Outreach

In addition to aggressive law enforcement, consumer education and outreach is an essential tool in our consumer protection and fraud prevention work. The Commission's education and outreach program reaches tens of millions of people a year,

---

[11] *FTC v. Goldman Schwartz, Inc.*, No. 4:13–cv–00106 (S.D. Tex. Jan. 14, 2013).
[12] *FTC v. NHS Systems, Inc.*, No. 09cv2215 (E.D. Pa. May 15, 2008).
[13] *See supra* note 2.
[14] *See FTC v. Am. Veterans Relief Foundation, Inc.*, No. CV09–3533 (C.D. Cal. June 3, 2009).
[15] This judgment was partially suspended based on the defendants' inability to pay the full amount.
[16] *See, e.g., FTC v. Matthew J. Loewen*, No. 12–CV–1207 MJP (W.D. Wa. Oct. 29, 2013) (Final Judgment and Permanent Injunction); FTC, *FTC Halts Two Automobile Dealers' Deceptive Ads*, Sept. 3, 2013, available at *http://www.ftc.gov/opa/2013/09/autoads.shtm;* FTC, *FTC Charges that Auto Loan Schemes Falsely Promised They Could Stop Consumers' Cars from Being Repossessed,* April 4, 2012, available at *http://ftc.gov/opa/2012/04/autoloans.shtm;* FTC, *FTC Charges Businesses Exposed Sensitive Information on Peer-to-Peer File-Sharing Networks, Putting Thousands of Consumers at Risk,* June 7, 2012, available at *http://www.ftc.gov/opa/2012/06/epn-franklin.shtm;* FTC, *FTC Takes Action To Stop Deceptive Car Dealership Ads,* Mar. 14, 2012, available at *http://www.ftc.gov/opa/2012/03/autoloans.shtm.*
[17] *See Public Roundtables: Protecting Consumers in the Sale and Leasing of Motor Vehicles,* Notice announcing public roundtables, requesting participation, and providing opportunity for comment, 76 Fed. Reg. 14014 (Mar. 15, 2011).
[18] The second roundtable particularly focused on these issues, and included several consumer military advocates on the discussion panels. Agendas, transcripts, and webcasts from the roundtables are available online. *See http://www.ftc.gov/bcp/workshops/motorvehicles.*
[19] *See http://ftc.gov/os/comments/motorvehicleroundtable/index.shtm.*

mostly through our websites, where people can access print, video, and audio information.[20] The FTC is widely known for its clear, understandable information and practical advice on dozens of consumer protection issues, including many issues affecting military consumers.

To better reach out to servicemembers and their relatives, the FTC maintains a *For Military Families* page on its consumer education website.[21] The page gathers the Commission's resources for servicemembers, veterans, and their families in one place to help them quickly find the consumer information of most use to them. These resources include materials that focus on the unique challenges faced by military families and emphasize the special rights that military families have when dealing with certain consumer protection issues. For example, the FTC released a consumer education post just a couple of weeks ago that provides information to veterans on how to avoid pitfalls in picking the right college.[22] The post includes advice on how to determine whether a school will provide credit for military training and how to find out more about the veteran-specific resources available from a school.

Some of the FTC's other military-specific resources include information on:

- understanding the protections that servicemembers and their dependents have with respect to payday loans (and certain other financing);[23]
- placing an active duty alert on a credit report, so as to better prevent creditors or collectors from attempting to collect a debt while a servicemember is overseas, in violation of the Servicemembers Civil Relief Act;[24]
- protecting personal information and limiting the harm from identity theft;[25]
- identifying dishonest pension advisors that try to bilk money out of veterans over 65 by providing poor (and often very harmful) advice about veteran's pensions;[26] and
- spotting and avoiding scams that claim to be soliciting donations to support military veterans and families of active-duty personnel.[27]

These resources comprise one component of the Commission's continuing effort to assist military communities in identifying, eliminating, and avoiding fraud.

To ensure that such educational materials have the maximum impact, we work with an extensive network of partnerships with other agencies, industry groups, consumer advocates, and community organizations to leverage resources and reach as many consumers as possible. For example, the FTC works with the DOD to disseminate articles, podcasts and blog posts using *MilitaryOneSource.mil* (a counseling hotline and website), military media, resource fairs, and other special projects.[28] Since 2009, the FTC has presented more than 30 podcasts and scores of webinars to servicemembers, their families, and the financial counselors that serve them.[29]

In the last several years, the FTC has expanded its existing partnerships with several military agencies and organizations, including the DOD and the CFPB. Staff from the FTC and these agencies meet regularly to discuss coordination and collaborative efforts. For example, the CFPB's Office of Servicemember Affairs shared the FTC's new article on how veterans can protect their pensions with hundreds of leaders in the military community.

---

[20] Consumer information can be found in English at *http://www.consumer.ftc.gov* and in Spanish at *http://www.consumidor.ftc.gov*.

[21] FTC Consumer Information, Military Families, available at *http://www.consumer.ftc.gov/features/feature-0009-military-families*.

[22] FTC Consumer Information, Choosing a College: 8 Questions to Ask, available at *http://www.consumer.ftc.gov/articles/0395-choosing-college*.

[23] FTC Consumer Information, Payday Loans, available at *http://www.consumer.ftc.gov/articles/0097-payday-loans*.

[24] FTC Consumer Information, Active Duty Alerts, available at *http://www.consumer.ftc.gov/articles/0273-active-duty-alerts*.

[25] FTC Consumer Information, Identity Theft: Military Personnel & Families, available at *http://www.consumer.ftc.gov/articles/pdf-0016-military-identity-theft.pdf*.

[26] FTC Consumer Information, Veterans' Pensions: Protect Your Money From Poachers, available at *http://www.consumer.ftc.gov/articles/0349-veterans-pensions*.

[27] FTC Consumer Information, Charitable Solicitations for Vet & Military Families, available at *http://www.consumer.ftc.gov/articles/0121-charitable-solicitations-vet-military-families*.

[28] For instance, in 2009 the Naval Criminal Investigative Services co-branded an FTC identity theft brochure and distributed 200,000 copies to naval personnel throughout the world as part of a three month program focusing on identity theft prevention and recovery.

[29] FTC staff have presented webinars for and recorded podcasts for servicemembers and families through DOD's MilitaryOneSource.mil; recorded podcasts and blog posts for DOD's Defense Media Directorate (New Media) and other military media; and presented webinars for DOD's contractors who provide financial counseling to the military community.

We are constantly searching for new and better ways to build on these partnerships. For instance, in 2012, the FTC launched a pilot program to improve our consumer protection outreach and assistance to military legal service personnel.[30] The program focused on the Navy's Mid-Atlantic Regional Legal Services Office, the largest of the U.S. Navy's commands. As part of the program, the FTC provided the Office with access to Consumer Sentinel as a law enforcement agency, established a dedicated e-mail contact at the FTC to enable the Office to receive timely assistance with consumer protection issues, and collaborated with the Office to create a 60 to 90 minute video loop of consumer protection materials. The FTC hopes that these efforts will help us create a blueprint for furthering our consumer protection outreach to the military.

More recently, the Commission and its partners—DOD, CFPB's Office of Servicemember Affairs, and Military Saves [31]—launched a campaign to empower servicemembers, veterans and their families with free consumer resources. On July 17 of this year, the FTC and other campaign organizers hosted "Military Consumer Protection Day 2013" to kick off the campaign.[32] As part of the campaign, the FTC created a website, *military.ncpw.gov,* that offers free tips and tools from government agencies, consumer and military advocacy groups, and non-profit organizations. The site is designed to inform the military community and veterans about consumer issues, such as managing money, dealing with credit and debt, building savings, making wise buying decisions, protecting personal information and avoiding fraud in the marketplace. We regularly update the site and blog with new information from the FTC and partners. Commanders, military financial counselors, and other trusted sources in the community can download or order materials and an outreach toolkit with a sample press release, newsletter article, flyer, and social media posts to help spread the word in the military and veteran communities. Planning is underway for Military Consumer Protection Day 2014 with a growing list of partners.[33]

The FTC also coordinates with its partners on military consumer protection policy initiatives. For example, the Commission is currently coordinating with the DOD via an interagency group on possible amendments to the DOD's military lending rule,[34] which would be issued pursuant to the recently amended Military Lending Act.[35] The Military Lending Act restricts covered loans, including certain payday loans by, for example, setting a 36 percent rate cap. Among other things, the amended Military Lending Act also establishes administrative and civil liability for violations, and gives the FTC enforcement authority for entities subject to its jurisdiction.[36] In addition to coordinating with DOD regarding that agency's possible amendments to their rule, the Commission's staff is reviewing complaints and other information for possible violations of these mandates.

---

[30] The project was part of the 2012–2013 FTC Excellence in Government Leadership Fellows Project, a leadership development program run by the Partnership for Public Service.

[31] Military Saves is a part of the DOD's Financial Readiness Campaign and has been a partner with DOD since 2003. Military Saves is a social marketing campaign to persuade, motivate, and encourage military families to save money every month, and to work with leaders and organizations to be aggressive in promoting automatic savings.

[32] FTC, *FTC, Partners to Kick Off First Military Consumer Protection Day July 17,* http://www.ftc.gov/opa/2013/07/mcpd.shtm.

[33] Other organizations that partnered on Military Consumer Protection Day 2013 included: Federal agencies (Department of Justice's Civil Division, Consumer Product Safety Commission, FINRA Investor Education Foundation, Food and Drug Administration, Department of Housing and Urban Development, Securities and Exchange Commission, Social Security Administration, U.S. Postal Inspection Service); state and local agencies (the offices of the Attorneys General of California, Colorado, Illinois, Massachusetts, New Mexico, North Carolina, Ohio, Washington, Hawaii and the Los Angeles County Department of Consumer Affairs); military and related organizations (Blue Star Families, National Association of Black Veterans, National Military Family Association, Coast Guard Office of Work-Life, Veterans Enterprises Service and Training); legal services (Pinetree Legal Assistance, Stateside Legal); consumer advocates (National Association of Consumer Advocates); and industry self-regulatory organizations (Better Business Bureau's Military Line, FINRA Investor Education Foundation, National Futures Association).

[34] Limitations on Terms of Consumer Credit Extended to Service Members and Dependents, 32 C.F.R. Part 232.

[35] *See* John Warner National Defense Authorization Act for Fiscal Year 2007 ("NDAA 2007" or "Military Lending Act"), Pub. L. 109–364, as amended by the National Defense Authorization Act for Fiscal Year 2013 ("NDAA 2013" or "amended Military Lending Act"), Pub. L. 112–239, codified in 10 U.S.C. § 987. Under the NDAA 2013, DOD is directed to consult with the Commission and other agencies at least every two years, in prescribing regulations under the Act. *See* 10 U.S.C. § 987(h)(3).

[36] *See* 10 U.S.C. § 987(f).

IV. Conclusion

The Commission will continue to take action to protect servicemembers and the broader military community from fraud and related threats and looks forward to working with you on this important issue.

The CHAIRMAN. Thank you, sir.

Ms. Deanna Nelson, Assistant Attorney General in charge of the Watertown Regional Office of the New York Attorney General's Office.

So can I call you General Nelson?

STATEMENT OF DEANNA R. NELSON, ASSISTANT ATTORNEY GENERAL IN CHARGE (WATERTOWN REGIONAL), STATE OF NEW YORK, OFFICE OF ATTORNEY GENERAL ERIC T. SCHNEIDERMAN

Ms. NELSON. You probably better not, Senator.

[Laughter.]

The CHAIRMAN. OK.

Assistant General Nelson?

[Laughter.]

The CHAIRMAN. All right. Deputy General Nelson, please.

Ms. NELSON. Thank you.

It is an honor to be here, Chairman Rockefeller and Ranking Member Thune and distinguished members of the Committee. This is a very important issue to Attorney General Schneiderman, and he is pleased that we can be represented on this panel.

My office sits outside the gates of Fort Drum, New York, which houses approximately 20,000 active military duty, families, soldiers. It's one of the most frequently deployed bases in the Nation. My office could probably spend all of its time focusing on consumer issues for soldiers because there are just so many different ways in which they're being victimized by unscrupulous businesses who are really only looking to make a buck.

One of the first and largest cases under my tenure of the office has been the SmartBuy case, and General Cooper accurately points out that these are the same cast of characters who were doing business in Tennessee.

As they were being shut down in Tennessee, they had changed their names and setup outside the gates of Fort Drum at our local mall under the name of SmartBuy. They had setup the exact same scheme, a beautiful marquee in the mall with lots of military focus. We would not have known that this was a problem in our area, but for the fact that soldiers had come into my office seeking help because they didn't know why the computer wasn't paid off yet.

I think that an important item for everyone on this committee to recognize is that sometimes these predatory lending products do not look predatory on their face. So when we initially looked at this contract we realized that it was showing an interest rate of approximately 19 percent. Anyone that has done this sort of work is used to seeing triple digits. So we didn't quite understand what was going on until we dug into the transaction itself.

I think this is an important consideration for the Committee and for other legislative bodies that are looking at the Military Lending Act, to say perhaps it's not the number; you have to look the transaction itself. And for example, in these SmartBuy transactions and many other transactions which target military, whether they're selling jewelry, whether their selling continuing education products, the devil is in the detail and you need look at the value of the underlying product.

What we had found was that the computer was merely the bait to get a soldier to sign on the dotted line. When we'd sent our consumer representative out to look at this marquee and see if we could get more clues as to what was going on, we realized that they wouldn't sell her a computer. She was an older woman who had worked with our office for a long time and they suggested she go to Wal-Mart, which was likely where they had purchased the computer in the first place.

As we called some of the staff of this organization into our office to get more details, we learned that's exactly what they were doing—buying these computers from Costco or Wal-Mart or Sam's club, remarketing them (just taking off the labels and putting on a new sticker so it appeared that it was something that they were selling directly), tripled the price, and then took the 19 percent interest on the inflated price. So, when we dug into the transaction itself, you realize that the computer may have been an $800 computer that was being sold for $2,400, but even that wasn't obvious to soldiers themselves because the prices were proprietary to these military per paycheck payment. So if he wanted to buy this computer, it might have been $60 per pay period or $120 per month, which seemed reasonable to them.

So as long as they could get that soldier to sign on the dotted line, setup an allotment payment, get their bank information—which could happen in less than 10 minutes—that's all that they were interested in doing. And they're not the only ones.

Looking around, just for this particular group of characters, we found them in multiple other states. We were able to shut them down in New York, but at the same time they were doing business in Texas, California, Colorado, North Carolina, South Carolina, Oklahoma, Georgia. And the point is, is that they were operating under different names in these places. So if you ran Britlee Incorporated in the Secretary of State's records for that state, you wouldn't find them. They had different names but the exact same scam.

The Attorney General wanted to make sure that this committee understood that you have to look at more than just the face of a contract and realize that $3,000 worth of debt is not secured by a $600 computer, and to make sure that going forward the regulations that are ultimately put into place are going to take into account the true nature of the transaction and understand that these scam artists, which is what they are, are going to find ways to redraft existing agreements so that they can continue to tap into those soldiers' paychecks and make sure that they get paid. They have something that they can sell and invest in.

So I'm very pleased that this committee is digging into this issue and is going to take steps to take care of our soldiers in this way because they're getting attacked on many different fronts.

Thank you very much for your attention on this matter.

[The prepared statement of Ms. Nelson follows:]

PREPARED STATEMENT OF DEANNA R. NELSON, ASSISTANT ATTORNEY GENERAL IN CHARGE (WATERTOWN REGIONAL), STATE OF NEW YORK, OFFICE OF ATTORNEY GENERAL ERIC T. SCHNEIDERMAN

General Schneiderman's Watertown Regional Office sits outside the gates of the 10th Mountain Division, Fort Drum, New York. Fort Drum is one of the most deployed Army bases in the country. It is a light infantry division, home to approximately 20,000-active duty soldiers.

A large proportion of the regional work involves assisting soldiers who have fallen victim to predatory lenders and other shady business practices. These same soldiers are also frequently the target of abusive collection tactics. Many times the soldiers' financial indignities have accrued over time from both online financial predators and unscrupulous businesses that target soldiers on posts across the country. These debts follow military families with each change in duty station, and often subject soldiers to sky-high interest accumulation upon return from deployment.

We are very sensitive to the fact that soldiers are different and more vulnerable than most other consumer groups:

- Soldiers' rate of pay is ascertainable by the marks on their uniform;
- Soldiers receive regular paychecks which can be tapped directly by allotment;
- There is no administrative recourse for a soldier once an allotment has been paid out;
- Soldiers are routinely requested to provide access to their commanders for collection efforts;
- If a soldier stops an allotment or challenges a contract, they are opening themselves to the possibility of disciplinary action, loss of rank or security clearance from their employers;
- Soldiers are moving frequently which makes it difficult to commence legal action or defend legal action on questionable or fraudulent "debts."
- Very often the fraud is not obvious on the face of the transaction, and neither the soldier nor command is in a ready position to raise an effective defense.

Basically, we are dealing with a very honorable class of victims who are not likely to cry foul once victimized.

The identified thread in the predatory lending market is a prevalence of unlicensed lenders or high-cost "military specialty" lenders. These businesses regularly have undisclosed or hidden costs, deceptively characterized loan/credit products, include subtle waivers of Fair Debt Collection Practices Act protections (*e.g.*, immediate access to chain of command), and engage in extremely aggressive collection/default activities.

These characteristics cross many markets targeting soldiers—electronics, furniture, jewelry, auto detailing/audio/upgrades, auto dealerships, "emergency" loans, leases, rent-to-own and other consumer products.

For purposes of this Committee's work, the focus of this submission will be anecdotal information regarding the anatomy of predatory behavior in these transactions—baiting, snagging and collecting.

All of the predatory businesses take time to identify their market and single them out. Typically they are draped in the American flag, many times they employ former servicemembers to heighten the trust of active duty soldiers, often times they hold themselves out as "specializing" in serving the needs of soldiers or Federal employees. The business may have given money to a military support organization in order to receive a certificate or plaque of appreciation, which are then prominently displayed at a business location or website—again, capitalizing on common affinity marketing techniques. These are all usual bait presented to our servicemembers, bait placed at the fingertips of our soldiers.

We have seen this in our litigation and investigations. The soldiers are targeted for the reasons cited above—they have paychecks, they will repay their debts, and they won't complain.

In one compelling example, the staff of a predatory business was trained to only sell to soldiers. When our office sent in a non-military staff member to explore purchasing from this business, she was directed to Walmart. The business was unwilling to sell its wares to anyone other than military, and refused any payment other than by allotment. In this particular instance, the business (located in the local mall), didn't even have a cash register or credit card reader at the store locations—only a stack of pre-filled finance agreements.

Some businesses are willing to accept non-allotment payment, but there typically is a very significant financing agreement accompanying the transaction, and usually some type of auto-payment required.

This should beg the question—what is the business selling?

This office has found time and again that the real product is not the truck, the computer, the education program, the sofa, the bedroom set, the auto detailing—it is the financing. And, as stated, the financing often comes directly out of the soldier's pay, with a back-up payment method already in place.

"Military paper" is how this class of product is described, and it generally bears no relationship to the value of the product financed, thereby maximizing profitability in a shadow industry which profits from this type of lending. There is a low entry cost and substantial profit.

What's an unlicensed lender? This is a class of private financing which is largely unregulated. It is not per se unauthorized, but it can be a black hole for consumers and treacherous territory for soldiers. On their face, the amounts are low. The interest rates are ostensibly capped. They are theoretically not payday loans because there is a tangible product passing hands. Nowhere on the paperwork is there any indication that the lender is anything other than a bank or a sanctioned loan company. The devil is in the detail.

In 2010 the New York Attorney General sued SmartBuy and two unlicensed, predatory lenders. These were the same cast of characters who had just been driven out of Tennessee, now operating under slightly different names. There was the bait—electronics, and the hook—financing. On its face, these were open-ended retail installment contracts from a lender, collateralized by the electronics sold. In reality, the outrageously high (and undisclosed) interest rates (over 200 percent) were stuffed into the "purchase price," making the stated interest rate appear to be within the range of predictable and authorized (10–12 percent). But there was underlying deceit: There were undisclosed loan costs associated with the required military allotment payment method. The full retail value of the product was never disclosed to the consumer. Sales persons soothed soldiers stating that the deals and interest rate were comparable to BestBuy. The soldier authorized the lender to contact command for a laundry list of issues, including collection. There was no way out of the contract even if a soldier wanted to return the product within the very short return period—there was a very expensive restocking fee which was required to be paid in cash. This type of contract skirts Military Lending Act protections, and also skirts lending laws.

Is overpayment a problem? Just because a soldier overpays—even dramatically—for a consumer good, does that mean there has been some sort of nefarious conduct? Likely, but not necessarily. Yet when the true price of a product has been buried in per paycheck price explanations, where the true effective interest rates are nowhere disclosed, where the contract deceptively bypasses existing state and Federal regulations by artfully framing the deal, consumers—and soldiers in particular—can be seriously hurt.

Have you ever pulled your current pay statement as part of a small consumer transaction? Short of purchasing a home or seeking a bank loan, it is safe to say that most of us have not. This is not the case for our service men and women. Routinely they are walked to a computer by vendors/lenders and asked to pull their LES (leave and earnings statement). Routinely they are asked for a copy of their military identification. Routinely they are asked to produce the name and contact information of their commander. When addressing soldiers as part of financial readiness training, I point out to them that this is not acceptable. They are stunned. It is a way of life for our soldiers.

As part of our SmartBuy investigation, an employee bragged to our undercover investigator that it was apparent after reviewing an LES, the soldier did not have sufficient unencumbered room for another allotment on his pay. The employee cancelled a different allotment in order to accommodate the new one. There is competition in this dark market.

As a resident near Fort Drum, I personally went into a rental car franchise to rent a vehicle. I presented my driver's license and a credit card and was handed a set of keys. At the same time, a young Army officer came in to rent a car. He was required to produce his driver's license, military identification, credit card, commander's name and contact information, and then was walked to a computer to print out his last LES. It is not right, and it cultivates the opportunity for predatory practices and abusive collection.

Time and again we are told that these soldiers have bad credit, that these are the best and only options available to them, and also that without the pressure of a command structure, they will not honor their debts. It is simply not true. The reality of the situation is that these soldiers are being deliberately placed between a rock and a hard place. The hard place is the collections practices.

When a debt goes into collection, it is a big problem for a soldier—they face potential disciplinary action, loss of rank, and potential loss of security clearances. Vendors know this, and they capitalize on the vulnerability.

The Fair Debt Collections Practices Act makes clear that debt collectors are not to contact third parties (read: employers) regarding a debt without express permission granted by the consumer, and the debt collector is further not permitted to utilize harassment, abuse, or false and misleading representations in the collection of any debt. In the experience of our office, these protections are routinely bypassed or disregarded.

These predatory contracts contain provisions permitting the lender to directly contact a soldier's chain of command to discuss the debt. Soldiers are routinely threatened that their command will be contacted. In some extreme instances, soldiers are threatened that military police will arrest them should they not recommence payment on debts. This form of terrorism is so prevalent that we've seen soldiers harassed for debts they have never even incurred—and many times they pay because the consequences of taking a stand are so consequential.

This situation presents problems for our soldiers, and also their commanders. I received a call from an officer on post, concerned that he was asked to respond and resolve problems on the "hotline." As he put it, he regularly received calls from businesses that soldiers were not paying on various debts, and there was only one part of that equation he had control over—the soldiers. We gave him some tools to push back.

The deception and the predatory behavior are not, however, obvious to anyone other than ourselves. We receive complaints from soldiers only when they cannot understand why they have already paid over $8,000 on a computer, but it is not paid off yet. We receive calls when a soldier is about to have security clearance terminated because of a debt they did not even know they had. We do not get complaints from soldiers that they have been paying illegal rates of interest, or were duped into a predatory transaction—they simply don't know.

The inevitable question arises: Is this a group of bad actors, or are there systemic failures, or both? In our experience, the answer is both. There are always "frequent fliers" who cultivate a degree of chaos which makes, for example, a move from Tennessee to New York nearly imperceptible, and which makes the transactions themselves appear legitimate to an uninformed reviewer. There are also abusive business and investment models which permit billions of dollars of fraud to evade regulatory oversight. These issues deserve our collective attention and redress. To this end, by letter dated June 23, 2013, Attorney General Schneiderman and several other attorneys general led by Delaware and Illinois, urged significant reform of the implementing regulations for the Military Lending Act. Large loopholes must be closed, including modifying the definitions of consumer credit to provide more comprehensive protections. The regulations must recapture loans which are open-ended or revolving, all auto title loans, any bank loan secured by funds on deposit, and all retail sales credit loans or other similar rent-to-own transactions. Similarly, age-old traditions such as payment by allotment must be revisited to review their efficacy in our modern age. What once was efficacious may now be simply a tool of abuse. The sanitizing role of regulatory oversight must also be considered—should billions of dollars of loan work be ignored simply because the victims are many and the individual loan amounts low? Clearly the answer is no.

Thank you for your attention to these abusive practices, and your dedication to protecting the brave men and women serving in our military.

The CHAIRMAN. Senator Nelson just said it is a crying shame. That's for sure.

Well, in the questions, I think we'll have some interesting discussion. Now, we come to——

Oh, no. See, now I'm all confused again because of here, retired Navy Captain—then I can't call you Mr. Dwain Alexander, can I?

I've got to call you Captain Alexander.

[Laughter.]

The CHAIRMAN. Please, we welcome your testimony.

**STATEMENT OF DWAIN ALEXANDER II,
SENIOR CIVILIAN ATTORNEY, REGION LEGAL SERVICE
OFFICE, MID-ATLANTIC, U.S. NAVY**

Captain ALEXANDER. Thank you, Mr. Chairman.

Chairman Rockefeller, Ranking Member Thune, and distinguished members of the Committee, I'm honored and humbled to have the privilege of representing the Navy's Judge Advocate General——

The CHAIRMAN. Excuse me, sir. Excuse me, sir.

I did not mention that you were Legal Assistance Attorney for the mid-Atlantic Region legal service office of the United States Navy.

Captain ALEXANDER. Thank you, sir.

I am honored and humbled to have the privilege of representing the Navy's Judge Advocate General's Corps and the servicemembers that we support.

I am a civilian Legal Assistance Attorney, and it's now called the Regional Legal Service Office. My job is to enhance sailor readiness by addressing legal issues and I want to, first, start off by thanking the members of the panel for all the fights that you give for the servicemembers that I see daily and for the tools that you give us to help us with our fight in the front. Thank you.

Consumer laws are the most complex and contentious issue that we address. Consumer issues attack the servicemembers finances impacting the individual, his family, unit morale, and, in the end, mission readiness and effectiveness. The cost of consumer issues on mission readiness is the loss of the expense, the training, and manpower investment that goes into each sailor along with his role in mission accomplishment.

I've had clients who purchase two cars in 1 day. It sounds perplexing but servicemembers have been trained to trust and follow authority and merchants know this and take advantage of that. In one case, I was able to cancel the contracts and the next day the Carrier Air Wing commander came to the base and to our command to thank us and to explain what that impact meant. He's the person on the aircraft carrier who is in charge of all the air operations. He said that I saved a crew member for him. The sailor was being trained to be a shooter on the deck of the aircraft carrier, that's the person that directs the planes to take off at the appropriate time.

In his experience, if a sailor had to pay for two vehicles, he would have no money. When his shipmates went out, he would not be able to go out and eventually he would begin to act out. This would become a disciplinary problem and, again in his experience, in 6 months they'd probably have to separate that servicemember and they'd lose the mission readiness that he provided by being part of their team. If he wasn't separated, the distraction of his finances could impact his job and the fighter jet that he directs on the flight deck of the aircraft carrier. For servicemembers, distractions can be dangerous and potentially fatal.

This sailor is not my only client. He's my typical client. They are all young, generally junior in rank, most only have a high school education. For them, their pay is guaranteed, it's recession-proof. So when the recession hit and cars couldn't be sold, my guys could buy cars. It's public knowledge, so when they go on into a business with a few questions, people know how much they make already. And their pay is easy to garnish. It's been mentioned they've been removed from their surroundings but that means that when they go to shop for a car, there's nobody to go with them and help them negotiate or say stop. Our sailors are transient; they move every 3 years. So there's no history that follows along saying this is a bad area or this is a bad business that isn't developed.

They've been trained to respect and respond to authority and that's critical for us in the military. When we ask somebody to swab a deck or to charge an enemy position, it's not a debatable issue. The problem is that for young people, that's not something they turn off. So when they go into a business and the retired somebody says, "You need to do this, I'm going to take care of you," they comply. And that compliance leads to financial troubles.

Their job is 24/7, it's a professional occupation. We regulate every aspect of their life, basically. And so, this is what they do and, for most of them, it's who they are. So when a debt collector calls the command or threatens to call the command and say, "I'm going to tell your commanding officer that you're a dead beat or you're not paying your bills," that has a very threatening impact. And I've had clients who have paid bills that they didn't owe but they had just arrived at the command or rather than have their names smudged before the commanding officer, they discharge their funds and paid the debt. That's just wrong. These factions combine to make the servicemember not only a high value target in the consumer market, but also very vulnerable to attack by unscrupulous actors.

I see four key challenges for servicemembers as consumers: Predatory lending, arbitration, Servicemember Civil Relief Act waivers, and aggressive debt collection. Thanks to the Military Lending Act and other agencies who have helped us with education and the education the Navy provides, we've done a very good job of educating servicemembers about payday loans and that they're not good things to do.

However, when there appears to be no other option, or the other options have been exhausted, they may get this loan. Knowing that it's the bad loan is the last thing that's going to report. And so, by the time we get an awareness of it, it's now a catastrophic event that's being dealt with and that again creates a problem for our readiness.

Beyond payday loans, though, automobile dealerships acting as loan brokers do far more damage that I think payday loans do. And most of the issues that I see in my practice in Norfolk are with the used car dealerships. There are a few franchise dealerships that create some issues for us, but used car dealerships are the primary ones.

This one time purchase can be devastating more devastating than a series of payday loans. The dealerships are located as close to the bases they can be. They will provide false information to lenders for the basic allowance for housing or the rank to increase the amount of money the servicemember can borrow placing them deeper in debt. The loans could be made for up to 140 percent of the vehicle's value, which allows them to pack along with all types of other accessory items. The dealers can receive kickbacks from lenders for higher interest rates. Vehicles can be a power—booked so they add in accessories or put them in zip codes where there's a higher value for the vehicle. Dealerships can require secondary loans to add money to the contract. This process makes our sailors the equivalent of a money delivery system for the automobile lending industry.

The same business would then include an arbitration provision in its contract. And we use this as a sword to fend off liability because servicemembers don't understand what arbitration is. They think that maybe I can see you in small claims court, but if you say, "You can't sue me, you signed an arbitration agreement," my sailors will just go away and pay the debt.

The last offense would be to add an SCR waiver, so that, like other businesses, the lender or dealer could get a default judgment without servicemember protections. The waiver of this orates the readiness protections or the Servicemember's Civil Relief Act.

Education will help avoid many debt traps. However, some problems like arbitration and the Servicemember's Civil Relief Act waiver and aggressive debt collection are beyond education. At my job, we are working with the Federal Trade Commission to develop videos that can be shown in the, hurry up and wait time; when in the lobby of the medical room or the supply or at legal, waiting for services, or you're returning from deployment, you can get education on consumer issues and we are feeding them that way and we are trying to take care of it. We have retired military training on payday loans and that's probably why part of those issues have been reduced.

We work with the Armed Forces Disciplinary Control Board to address unscrupulous businesses to the best of our ability. But still, these problems create such a hazard for servicemembers and some of the issues the servicemember's waiver in the arbitration being in the contracts, are things that we can't address because they're legal. So we need help to deal with that.

Thank you.

[The prepared statement of Captain Alexander follows:]

PREPARED STATEMENT OF DWAIN ALEXANDER II, SENIOR CIVILIAN ATTORNEY, REGION LEGAL SERVICE OFFICE, MID-ATLANTIC, UNITED STATES NAVY

Chairman Rockefeller, Ranking Member Thune, and distinguished members of this Committee, as a legal assistance attorney in the United States Navy, I am honored and humbled to have the privilege of representing the Navy's Judge Advocate General's Corps and the servicemembers we support.

I am a civilian legal assistance attorney, who, like all uniformed and civilian legal assistance attorneys, works to support and enhance sailor and mission readiness by addressing their legal readiness issues.

Legal issues can be very distracting for many individuals. But for active duty servicemembers, legal distractions can be dangerous and potentially fatal. We need our servicemen and women focused on their primary mission—national defense. Legal assistance services that we provide include estate planning, family law and consumer law. Between these areas of practice, we cover the majority of servicemember legal readiness needs.

For estate planning services, we draft documents that ensure servicemembers' final wishes are expressed. For family law matters, we provide advice and counsel on a wide range of domestic topics to help servicemembers and dependents understand their legal rights and responsibilities. For consumer law, we engage opposing parties, explain the law, and the servicemembers' rights. Consumer law stands out as the most complex and contentious. Of the three broad areas of legal assistance, consumer law matters attack servicemembers' finances. This can have a negative impact on the individual, his family, his personal and unit morale, and in the end, mission readiness and effectiveness. This reflects the reality that while our clients have the desire and ability to engage in commerce as a consumer—and engage they do, the majority of our clients are young and lack the necessary financial savvy needed to avoid some consumer traps.

I once had a client who purchased two vehicles in one day. While this may sound perplexing, consider military psychology. Servicemembers have been trained to follow authority. If someone appearing to act with authority tells you something you want to hear like, "the first vehicle was from a bad dealer and you could get into trouble for buying it" or "the contract is not final because you have temporary plates," and "I'm a retired master sergeant—I will take care of you and return your car so you can buy mine." Our experience indicates that there is a very good chance that servicemember will comply and become liable for a second financial obligation. This situation is unsustainable.

In this particular case, I was able to cancel both contracts. The next day the Carrier Air Wing Commander came in to thank me and explain the impact to his mission. He said that I saved a crew member. The sailor was being trained to be a shooter on the deck of an air craft carrier. If he had to pay for two vehicles, he would not have any money. When his shipmates went out he could not go. He would be working just to pay bills and would begin to act out. He would become a disciplinary problem, and in six months they would probably have to separate him. The negative impact of consumer law on mission readiness is that the expense, training and manpower investment the sailor represents is lost, as is his role in mission accomplishment.

This sailor is my typical consumer client. They are young and the majority are junior in rank. Most have only a high school education. Their pay is guaranteed—recession proof, furlough proof, public knowledge, and easy to garnish. They have been removed from familiar surroundings and family support systems, and have been trained to respect and respond to authority—a critical mindset that is vital to the operation of the military. To illustrate—whether we ask the sailor to swab the deck or charge an enemy position, there is no option for open debate. Our sailors are transient, moving every two to three years, so little history of the consumer environment is retained and passed on. Their job is a 24/7 professional occupation and an integral part of their life. Threats by merchants to contact their command with assertions of breach of contract or debt dodging reflect on their conduct and judgment and are perceived as potentially career ending. These factors combine to make the servicemember not only a "high value target" in the consumer market place, but also very vulnerable to attack by unscrupulous actors.

The key weapons I see used against servicemembers in my practice are: Predatory lending, arbitration clauses, Servicemembers Civil Relief Act waivers, and aggressive debt collection.

There are many predatory lending schemes—from the traditional "payday lenders", to predatory lending related to the automobile industry. Consumer education on pay day lenders has reduced the negative impacts on our clients. However, an emergency or a few bad financial decisions and the payday "non-loan" may appear to be a good option. Another type of predatory lending loans procured automobile dealerships acting as loan brokers. Loan applications made by dealerships can contain false information increasing the income of the servicemember. These loans can be for up to 140 percent of vehicle's value. The dealerships can receive kickbacks from lenders in the forms of finance charge sharing. Vehicles can be "power booked" to artificially increase its value. When the primary and secondary market will not provide sufficient funds dealerships can require supplemental secondary loans to add money to the contract. This process makes our sailors the equivalent of a money delivery system to the auto and lending industry. I had a client who purchased a vehicle for $11,000.00, the max loan amount from the traditional creditor. The dealer wanted more money for the vehicle so he sold the client a dash mounted GPS for $2500.00 financed through a secondary subprime lender. Other clients are told that additional funds are needed for taxes. In another case the dealership sold the vehicle for $5,700.00 but added on a service contract for $3,069.00.

Arbitration is another area of concern. The issue with the arbitration is that many servicemembers will not pursue their rights. Arbitration can have high costs and require hearings in inconvenient forums. It is also an unknown process to the servicemember consumer. They do not know the law and when told, "you cannot sue me because you signed an arbitration agreement" they may not pursue their claim. Many auto dealerships have arbitration provisions in their contracts. I recently saw a case in which the sailor purchased a vehicle "As-Is." He made extensive inquiries about the condition of the vehicle prior to purchase and was informed it was in good condition. After purchase he found the vehicle had substantial damage that should have been disclosed under the Federal Trade Commission's Buyers Guide. The contract had an arbitration provision. This dealership used the arbitration provision to avoid liability. Arbitration is essentially a waiver of the servicemembers right to expeditiously resolve matters in trial. In Virginia most of these issues could be addressed in small claims or general district court in 45 days at a cost of $48.00. General District Court has a jurisdictional of cap of $25,000.00.

The Servicemember's Civil Relief Act is a great consumer protection statute for the military. It acknowledges the importance of the servicemember's focus on the mission and provides tools to balance the Nation's interest in national security with individual rights. It places aspects of civil law matters that could impact mission readiness in the hands of commands and servicemembers. However, one section exception eviscerates any protections; the Section 517 Waiver. The unlimited and unconditioned use of the waiver takes readiness out of the hands of servicemembers and commanders and places it in the hands of landlords and merchants. In Virginia there is a standard form lease, VAR 200. This is a 14 page residential lease that provides a reservation of right by the landlord to require a waiver of the SCRA at a later time. There are also countless other waiver forms with waivers ranging from total to single item like default protection (Section 521), eviction protection (Section 531) or Lease termination (Section 535). As an attorney, I can argue the inapplicability or unlawful nature of the waiver based upon the knowledge at the time of execution and the involuntary nature of the contract provision; my clients will not. They will honorably acknowledge that they signed a waiver and accept the penalty.

Once there is an obligation the servicemember can fall prey to aggressive debt collection procedures. The type of collection process will usually include threats to contact the command or actually contact with the command. Because of the importance of the security clearance and the competitive nature of promotion, negative comments to a servicemember's command will be perceived by the servicemember as a threat to his or her career in the Navy. This gives creditors great leverage with collections of valid and invalid obligations. For example, one client who had transferred from the west to the east coast had settled an obligation with a creditor. That debt was resold to another collection company who contacted the servicemember. He had just moved and could not find his paperwork. Rather than have the creditor contact his command, as they had threatened, he paid them $1,000.00.

There are two keys to addressing the problems protection and education. No amount of education can address the arbitration provision or waiver when the use is legal and pervasive. A decision between signing a waiver with this landlord or living far away or in an unsafe area is a choice between two bad options. With arbitration there frequently is no choice. The perception that aggressive debt collection will impact a servicemember's career is very real to the servicemember. Knowing your rights is the first step in meaningful participation in a market economy. My office is working with the FTC to make their library of informative videos on consumer law available to servicemembers in infomercial format in lobbies, waiting rooms, and on ships so that while sailors are waiting for the next evolution in their day they can receive consumer law tips. We also provide symposiums on consumer law for military attorneys, financial counselors and servicemembers.

We are doing our best to educate on their rights and to protect servicemembers when their rights are violated. It is important that the law provide the tools necessary to allow servicemembers and those who fight for servicemembers to win in an engagement where the enemy is consistently changing.

Mr. Dwain Alexander II

Mr. Alexander is the senior supervisory civilian attorney and subject matter expert for the Region Legal Service Office, Mid Atlantic in Norfolk Virginia.

He is a native of Kansas City, Missouri. He earned his Bachelor of Science Degree from Creighton University in 1982 and his Juris Doctor from Creighton University School of Law in 1989. After law school he joined the Navy Judge Advocate General's Corps.

Mr. Alexander left active duty in 1996 and affiliated with the Reserves where he attained the rank of Captain. He retired from the United States Navy in September of 2013.

At the Region Legal Service Office, Mid-Atlantic, Mr. Alexander is responsible for legal assistance program development, where he tracks local, state, and Federal legislation impacting the provision of legal services. He provides comments on legislation and agency rulemaking and drafts legislative proposals related to the covered areas of practice. He develops and maintains inter-service and civilian partnership programs with the American Bar Association, the Armed Forces Disciplinary Control Board, the National Association of Consumer Advocates, the National Consumer Law Center, the Virginia State Bar, and local Bar Associations. He mentors, trains, and contributes to the professional development of enlisted and staff attorneys at the Navy's largest Region Legal Service Office. Mr. Alexander also provides legal services to servicemembers and their families. His primary areas of practice are estate planning, consumer law, and family law. He has represented thousands of clients over his 24 years of service with the Navy. Mr. Alexander is a frequent speaker at conferences and legal education courses. He is a subject matter expert on servicemembers' rights, the Servicemembers Civil Relief Act, automobile transactions and automobile fraud.

Mr. Alexander is the consumer law advisor for the Navy Region Mid-Atlantic, Armed Forces Disciplinary Control Board. He is a member of the American Bar Association's Standing Committee on Legal Assistance for Military Personnel and currently serves as Chair of the Military Law Section of the Virginia State Bar and Co-Chair of the National Association of Consumer Advocates, Military Consumer Justice Project. He is a contributing author for several legal publications, including the National Consumer Law Center's publication on *Collection Actions* and the American Bar Association's *Legal Guide for Military Families.*

The CHAIRMAN. Thank you very much, sir.

I'm going to ask Ms. Petraeus and Mr. Harwood a question, but I almost question my question before I ask it.

I want you to talk a little bit about what, I mean, you've all talked about, most of you, about the vulnerability, the young age. There are families who are in the process of moving, they're going back overseas again, the soldier is, again, so, I mean, there's confusion. You know, people don't understand the terminology; they're not accustomed to dealing with them. And I'm just looking at some of the ads that these companies send out and they all look like they were, you know, representatives working right out of Chuck Hagel's office. I mean, they're all military and they're all serving U.S. military around the world since 1999. And then they have a testimony from one very wonderful-looking woman soldier, and she says, "After there was a mistake with my pay, I didn't know how to make ends meet." So you're with her, right? "Luckily, they understood my situation and were willing to help me when I needed it. Thanks for helping me." Well, here it is, written. And people are going to fall for that. They're going to fall for that.

So my question to you, Ms. Petraeus and Mr. Harwood—two different consumer protection agencies, so to speak—what can you do in outreach and education? What is it really possible to do? I mean, these folks are changing, they get a video display or whatever; I mean, how can you really reach them?

Ms. PETRAEUS. Well, Chairman, I think you're always going to have to have a combination of both education and protection. When it does come to education and outreach, there are a variety of things that can be done. I think you've heard some today. We are doing our best, at our agency, to do kind of a combination of things. I personally have gone to 70 different military installations, in part, to put a face on the bureau and what we do. I ask to hear about their financial issues, but if it is a large group of young servicemembers, I also throw in a little bit of consumer protection common sense when I talk to them as well. We are developing some education products, one to be delivered even before they get to basic training because basic training is kind of a stressful time to absorb good financial education; you're tired, you're stressed, you're scared of the drill instructor and you may just not be hearing that good information. So, we're going to do a little product that can be accessed by computer before they even get there with some basic common sense——

The CHAIRMAN. But what would be the setting for that? I mean, they would be out in the field practicing marksmanship, or do they——

Ms. PETRAEUS. No, no. The delayed entry is when they've committed to join the military but they have not yet gone to boot camp.

The CHAIRMAN. Oh.

Ms. PETRAEUS. So the only contact they really have at that point is with their recruiter. And we will work with the Department of Defense so the recruiter will deliver to them this website, go to this website, take this short financial course and show me that you did it. So we're hoping, again, to catch them before they even get that first military paycheck or get that first trip to the local mall when they're at basic training and may be tempted by that kiosk that they find there.

So we're hoping that's one approach that might help. We are also working, certainly, with other Federal and State agencies. I've had 16 state attorneys general go with me personally to military installations to say, we are here to protect you in this state as consumers. We work with the FTC, as you've heard. I've worked with the National Conference of State Legislatures and a number of the non-profits that play in the military space.

We're also doing some train the trainer efforts from our office, doing webinar video events for those who deal with military issues like the financial program managers, the JAGs and the education service officers, trying to give them the latest information about current rules and regulations that are in effect. We have a military listserv, we, you know, put out regular publications. We also helped re-write the Transition Assistance Program for those who are transitioning out of the military.

So there are a variety of things that can be done. We can always do more, we can always do better and again, education is essential, but I think it does have to be combined with the protection of loss as well.

The CHAIRMAN. Protection of rules and regulation or protection of loss?

Ms. PETRAEUS. Yes. All of the above.

The CHAIRMAN. OK.

Mr. HARWOOD. I couldn't agree more with what Ms. Petraeus said. I think tackling this problem is a combination of education and law enforcement. And, you know, on the law enforcement side, I can tell you that there are some laws and rules that already would apply to misrepresenting affiliation with the military. I talked about a case at the FTC filed this summer involving Mortgage Investors Corp. in which they misrepresented they were affiliated with the VA in connection with the loans that they were issuing. Those misrepresentations violated the Mortgage Advertising Practices Act and that obviously—to have that language in there was helpful in our law enforcement efforts.

Representations about affiliation—misrepresenting affiliations with a government agency or military entity would also violate the Mortgage Assistance Relief Services Rule that the FTC recently promulgated, or was actually promulgated several years ago. Both those rules still are enforceable by the FTC. They were also, actually, they've been transferred down to CFPB and the CFPB also has the authority to enforce both those rules. And affiliations like the kind we're talking about except affiliations that would be in violation of those. More generally, on the enforcement side, a representation about being affiliated with a government entity when the scammer is not would violate the FTC Act and we've had cases over the years that involve that as well.

So all of those things are, that's the law enforcement side. And it's obviously critically important to do that because you're right, and I think you alluded this in your question. The problem is that by representing they're somehow, these folks are somehow affiliated with a legitimate agency, they get instant credibility with the consumers, in this case, military consumers, and they may well let their guard down and not be as aggressive in terms of the questions they might ask and not be as attuned to the, you know, to, sort of, some of the educational messages that we normally would try to get them to think about.

But education is also still an important part. And I think you asked Ms. Petraeus about some of the educational efforts we've made. I actually wanted to go back to something that Mr. Alexander mentioned where he talked about one of our new educational initiatives we've been experimenting with, specifically in Norfolk, and that is the idea that we can use wait time in the military. It turns out that servicemembers spend a lot of time waiting and not doing a lot except waiting. And the idea that we've been working on with, actually, with Mr. Alexander, closely, is the idea we can use those wait time opportunities to deliver educational messages about a variety of scams and problems we're seeing. And, you know, through videos in waiting rooms, on ships as they're coming back into shore, those are all great opportunities for us to, with Mr. Alexander's help and the help of his organization, to let soldiers know about the kinds—and sailors, in this case, know about the kinds of scams that may be targeting them, including scams that are purporting to be affiliated with the military. Thank you.

The CHAIRMAN. I hear you, but I'm trying to think of these soldiers. I mean, you don't really learn how people can take advantage of you until they have taken advantage of you and you lost your security, you know, the three cars that you paid for you never bought. I mean, you have to go through it. I'm not sure it's in the nature of 22-year-olds and 25-year-olds who are, you know, in the middle of preparations for war, going back to war, that sort of a discussion, a lecture in a waiting room—I'll get to you, sir. On his time, though.

[Laughter.]

The CHAIRMAN. Because I'm taking all of his time already. That they'll listen, they'll learn, but will it actually make them sharp when confronted by these scumbags, as I would call them? And so what I was thinking is, are we doing it the right way? In other words, if you have all of these service men and women, all potential victims, all going to be in these camps, military camps, surrounded, as you say, surrounded by SmartBuys, my new favorite company. Why can't we go after, General—well, I just asked a question and then John Thune can do whatever he wants with it.

Go after the perpetrators. I remember during the health insurance matters in this committee. We had these outrageous charges being charged on, you know, sophisticated, unsophisticated people. And it wasn't really until we ran into a little group called Ingenix, which nobody had ever heard of, which turned out that they were sort of setting the rates for all insurance companies all across the country but people didn't want to admit it. When they got taken to court in the City of New York, I believe, maybe state of New York, and they ended up paying, I think, $350 million, that, I think, SmartBuy might understand.

So it's a question of human nature evolving into sufficient sophistication. Or is it a question of us jumping on the perpetrators with a clear track record of who they might be at the proper time? And actually, you don't even have to answer that, because I'm 5 minutes over my time. So Senator Thune will carry on.

[Laughter.]

Senator THUNE. You're just getting rolling, Mr. Chairman.

The CHAIRMAN. I know, I was.

[Laughter.]

Senator THUNE. Thank you.

Captain Alexander, my understanding is that the Armed Forces Disciplinary Control Board identifies to base commanders businesses that may be especially harmful to servicemembers and places such businesses off-limits to servicemembers. Can you elaborate how you work with the board to identify businesses that may be placed on the off-limits list?

Captain ALEXANDER. Yes, sir.

We have a consumer complaint form that we have sent out to all the commands in the area, so whether it's a command financial specialist at the command advising the servicemember on an issue that they see, are they coming to our office? The first step is to document what the problem is by putting it on that form. The front part of that form is also the notification to the Armed Forces Disciplinary Control Board that there is a problem. The precepts of the Board say we can't take on individual issues, so we can't take on this sailor's case, but if we get three or four or a very egregious act that we think could be impacting multiple servicemembers, then the board will send an invitation for that party to come forth and explain what the process is. This is one of the reasons why we've been very successful in addressing some of the car dealers in our area is that when you put one car dealer off-limits, their sales may drop from 40 or 60 cars a month to 12 and that impacts their bottom line and then they begin to think about restructuring the way they do their processes. So we work with the Board carefully in doing that, in documenting the cases and then in bringing them to the Board for action against individual businesses that are causing problems, sir.

Senator THUNE. Ms. Petraeus, thank you, by the way for your personal visits. You mentioned in your testimony that during your visits to different bases, issues related to high-cost lending come up at nearly every stop. And I'm wondering if the CFPB has collected or released any statistics on the number of servicemembers affected by these issues, and what does the data suggest or reflect in terms of trends in the past few years? Is this problem getting much worse? Has it stayed the same?

Ms. PETRAEUS. We are a young agency, so our data is —what we've found out from our complaints that have been filed with us by servicemembers, we've gotten, at this point, just over 11,000 complaints from servicemembers and mortgages top the list, challenges with mortgages. But we only started taking complaints about debt collection several months ago and that's already trending upwards so fast, it's the number two complaint item that we're getting. So I think there's definitely a sign there that that is something that impacts servicemembers quite a bit.

And in fact, it's rather timely because we just did put out an advance notice of proposal we're making on debt collection and we are soliciting comments from the public through the 10th of February, so we certainly are very interested in having a military component to the comments that we receive. Because anecdotally and from what we've gotten in our military complaints, it's pretty obvious that debt collection is one of the biggest challenges that servicemembers seem to be impacted by.

Senator THUNE. And do you see, from base to base or state to state, differences? And what do you attribute those to if you do?

Ms. PETRAEUS. It would be hard for me to expound on that right now. I think, certainly, I see differences between some of the issues that impact, for example, the National Guard, the Reserves, versus active duty. They're definitely more impacted by employment issues and GI Bill issues; heavily marketed to by for-profit colleges. When they go to use their GI Bill, that's something that we've heard a lot about from the Guard.

So, state by state, we could certainly take a look at the complaints and get back to you on that, but I haven't seen any, you know, any dramatic differences from one state to the next.

Senator THUNE. OK. Do you work with the Bureau's Office of Consumer Response to encourage servicemembers to file complaints regarding their concerns and then to help ensure the resolution of those complaints from servicemembers?

Ms. PETRAEUS. Yes, very much so. I do have two folks within my office working on consumer response issues. One of them pretty much does a full-time job working with the Office of Consumer Response. She is a recent Army JAG, so she's a really excellent person to be doing this because she has a real knowledge of the laws that affect the military and can be value added, both in their review of complaints that come through but also in training up our Consumer Response folks on some of the military-specific issues that may come in with complaints.

Senator THUNE. And does the CFPB share the information about these complaints with military officials?

Ms. PETRAEUS. If there's a Servicemembers Civil Relief Act component, especially since that's something we don't enforce, we do share that with DOD and the Department of Justice, Civil Rights Division. We have a real three-way conversation with them. In fact, one of the first things we did was sign a joint statement of principles with those two entities so we would be sure that there were no military complaints that would fall through the cracks just because it wasn't an area that we specifically covered.

Senator THUNE. OK.

And I would just direct this to the panel in its entirety and whoever would like to answer, but not all short-term loans are, by definition, predatory. So if a servicemember is looking for a short-term loan, what types of things should they be on the lookout for?

Mr. COOPER. Ranking Member Thune, I would suggest a couple of things.

Obviously, in a transactional situation where there is high-pressure sales tactics, that ought to be a red flag. If it's a you have to sign now or you'll lose the deal, then that's clearly a red flag. And I would encourage a servicemember who is presented with any sort of contract or finance agreement that in any way is confusing to ask for the opportunity to take it back to the base and have someone look at it. And if the merchant's unwilling to do that, I would say that's a very big red flag.

Senator THUNE. All right.

Anyone else want to add anything else to that?

Ms. PETRAEUS. I'd like to just weigh in.

The first thing that they sometimes forget to consider is that every branch of the service has a Military Relief Society that makes emergency loans and grants at zero percent interest. So if it's a true emergency, that should be the first place they're looking. And sadly, sometimes it's not. In fact, when I was up at Fort Drum, we had a young soldier who just got up at the Town Hall to tell his story, which was that he needed a loan, it was a family emergency, he didn't even think to go on-post; he went on the Internet. And he got a horribly expensive loan and ended up paying more in fees than the loan was actually for and he could've gotten a zero-interest loan had he known to go on-post. So that's the first place I would like them to look if it's a true emergency. Obviously, possibly their on-base bank or credit union would be another source of a loan at reasonable rates.

But definitely what I don't want them to be doing is trolling the Internet and looking for one of those tens of thousands or even millions of offers that offer military loans——

Senator THUNE. Right.

Ms. PETRAEUS.—and are very bad deals.

Senator THUNE. OK. Thank you.

Thank you, Mr. Chairman.

The CHAIRMAN. Thank you, Senator Thune.

Senator Ayotte?

STATEMENT OF HON. KELLY AYOTTE, U.S. SENATOR FROM NEW HAMPSHIRE

Senator AYOTTE. Thank you, Mr. Chairman. I want to thank you and the Ranking Member for this important hearing and all of you for being here.

And it's good to see you, General Cooper. We had the opportunity to serve together when I was New Hampshire AG. I wanted to ask you as an Attorney General: This issue came to my attention as well. In fact, New Hampshire made the decision, while I was Attorney General, to cap the interest rates at 36 percent because there were examples of payday-type loans where people were paying as high as 500 percent. And so, I was very interested, as I looked at your testimony, about the case that you brought against Rome Finance and Britlee. Did you do that under the Consumer Protection Act as an unfair and deceptive practice? That is a tool that many attorneys general have and I wondered if you felt that was a sufficient tool? Many of the attorneys general were using this tool to try to go after businesses within their jurisdiction that were using these predatory lending practices.

Mr. COOPER. Yes, Senator Ayotte, very good to see you again also, and enjoyed very much serving with you as fellow state AGs.

And yes, to answer your question, our lawsuit was brought under our Tennessee Consumer Protection Act, saying that these practices were false and misleading.

Senator AYOTTE. And how is that? Has that been a good tool for AGs? Is it a sufficient enough tool? And I guess I'll pose, as well, to others on the panel here. The way I see this right now, we've got the authority of the state AGs under their Consumer Protection Act; you've got action that the FTC could take; and then we now have the CFPB working on this issue—Ms. Petraeus, thank you for everything that you're doing on this.

And so, how do the three fit together to make sure that we're maximizing our coordination? I know all of you were talking about education and I fully agree. Part of what we do on our Consumer Protection Act is just make examples of people so that other people can understand not to fall for a scam or not to be put in a situation that is bad, particularly for our men and women in uniform. So I just wanted to get all of your thoughts. Do you think the Consumer Protection Act is a good vehicle at the state level? And then, what do you think about the three agencies working together to make sure that we're doing the right thing, and we're getting the message out?

Mr. COOPER. Yes, I suspect that the effectiveness of the State Consumer Protection Acts will vary from state to state. We find ours to be a very effective tool, both in terms of, you know, what it prohibits at the state level. And we also take the position that, you know, where action also violates a comparable Federal statute, the MLA or something else, that that would also be a violation of the state law because it is in violation of the Federal law. And that, I guess, leads——

Senator AYOTTE. Can you also get treble damages and some——

Mr. COOPER. Yes, we also get treble damages where we have the ability to seek injunctive relief, to seek restitution. So we have a variety of tools in that tool bag. But we do work closely with the FTC, with the CFPB, whenever we can partner with a Federal partner particularly on, as we encounter more and more of these companies that are national in scope. And where, you know, we need to go all over the Nation to pursue it, that it's so much easier and so much more effective when we can do that with the FTC or do that with the CFPB or our other Federal agencies.

Senator AYOTTE. Ms. Petraeus, Mr. Harwood, how do you see us all interacting together on such an important issue?

Ms. PETRAEUS. Well, I think you're absolutely right; we should be working in harness as best we can. Again, I certainly value what the AGs do at the state level. And sometimes state laws may go farther than the Federal law and they can be very effective and that's part of why I attempt to horn in on their conferences whenever I can and talk to them and remind them what we do. We also have certainly partnered with the FTC. The FTC and the CFPB did a joint sweep of some really egregious mortgage advertisements that resulted in a number of warning letters and also some potential future enforcement actions. So I think we can be very effective together and also in combination with you. And there are gaps in the law where things aren't covered, either at the state or the Federal level.

Mr. HARWOOD. I mean, I would just second or third, I guess, what the others have said.

My experience has been that on all levels, cooperation has been very strong. In terms of information sharing, the FTC's consumer complaint database is shared widely with state attorneys general, with the CFPB. Data that goes in from us is available to CFPB, it's available to state attorneys general; indeed, it's available to military law enforcement.

Second, with regard to enforcement efforts, there's a long history of joint enforcement efforts. As I was sitting here, I was reminded of some work that I worked on in 2009 that involved deceptive charity scams, and some of which were related to raising money for military causes. That sweep, which we announced in mid-2009, involved multiple state efforts. It was a great example of where states had more authority than we did in some situations because they have a better—they have stronger charities laws, so they targeted the scam charities and we targeted some of the fundraisers that were engaged in that.

Senator AYOTTE. I'm glad you raised that point. I know my time is up, but you're absolutely right because, for example, when I served as Attorney General, I had a consumer protection bureau, I had a charitable bureau as well that had authority to regulate charities. So the two working together can give greater authority sometimes under state law and I'm glad to hear that we're looking to see which agency is the best to deal with to make sure that we hold these people accountable and then get the message out to let people know that these bad actors are out there and they shouldn't go down that road. Thank you.

The CHAIRMAN. Thank you, Senator Ayotte.

We have been joined by Senator Markey.

STATEMENT OF HON. EDWARD MARKEY, U.S. SENATOR FROM MASSACHUSETTS

Senator MARKEY. Thank you, Mr. Chairman, very much. And thank you for holding this very important hearing, you know, because people who serve us in the military, they're heroes, but heroes need help, you know? They make us secure but they actually live with insecurity in terms of their own personal financial circumstances.

And so we have a responsibility to put in place the kinds of programs that help to ensure that that security is there and we have to make sure that there's a safety net ready so that they don't have to run to predatory payday lenders. And I think that's something that I'd like to talk a little bit about here today because members of our military have to resort to financing from these predatory lenders all too often.

We know that military servicemembers are three times more likely than civilians to use predatory payday loans that charge exorbitant rates that's three times what civilians use. Twenty-seven percent of military families carry $10,000 or more in credit card debt compared to only 16 percent for civilian families. Ten percent of military families carry more than $20,000 in debt compared to only seven percent of civilian families. And more than half of military servicemembers are not saving for the future and have trouble paying their monthly bills.

And that's why, this morning, I reintroduced my Military Savings Act, which is legislation I previously introduced in the House of Representatives. And the bill would promote savings rates among military servicemembers and decrease their need to turn to predatory payday lenders in times of financial crisis. The bill establishes a pilot program in which financial institutions operating on military bases will offer innovative financial products to help troops and their families improve their financial situations. And they can include a new kind of savings account that automatically deposits a portion of their additional income that the servicemember earns while on deployment into a savings account rather than going entirely into a checking account. And that bill has now been endorsed by the Consumer Federation of America.

So, Ms. Petraeus, I'd just like to ask you: What is your feeling about a program like that, that could be put in place in order to give additional protections for servicemembers?

Ms. PETRAEUS. Well, Senator, thank you for your concern for military and their families and the financial challenges that they do face.

I think anything that promotes innovative products that will help them save is a good thing. And we did hold a Financial Fitness Forum about 6 months after I started at the CFPB to get some best practices from some of the financial institutions that serve the military. And I was certainly very interested in the ones that combined both, you know, a fair deal with a potential savings component. Because the truth is, if you need to borrow it today and you're not saving anything for the next time, you're going to be out there borrowing it again and we need to work on anything we can to help break that cycle of repeated borrowing and never setting anything aside.

So I look forward to seeing that, the results of a pilot like this.

Senator MARKEY. Thank you.

Mr. Harwood, your views on a pilot project like——

Mr. HARWOOD. I find the idea to be very intriguing. The idea that you would, you know, be with, through legislation, encourage a broader range of financial products and services on these installations. Obviously, the FTC is both a consumer protection and a trust agency. On the trust side, we love competition, we love to see more options available for consumers, we love to see, for example, our choices. This would do that.

Senator MARKEY. Thank you.

Mr. HARWOOD. Yes.

Senator MARKEY. Any other comments from other of the panelists, in terms of creating that kind of a program for servicemembers? Ms. Nelson?

Ms. NELSON. I think, obviously, a variety of products is a fabulous idea and I think that's a really great step, Senator. And I think that transparency of these products, too, which seems to be lacking in a lot of financial products soldiers are looking at, is going to be a key component to the success of something like that so that the soldiers can easily compare, make wise consumer decisions, and not get themselves in problems down the road.

So I think that is an excellent idea in terms of creating the diversity.

Senator MARKEY. Thank you.

Anyone else? Yes, Mr. Cooper.

Mr. COOPER. Yes, Senator Markey, no, I think I would just add my voice to these that anything we can do, as we've discussed before in terms of promoting financial literacy and education among the troop members will be of great benefit to them and to morale and to the effectiveness of the troops.

So I think this is a wonderful idea.

Senator MARKEY. Good. Thank you so much.

So, I thank you, Mr. Chairman. I think this is a very important subject area. We know that this is a real problem out there. And we know that three million people have served in the Iraq wars and Afghanistan, which is unbelievable, the number is so huge. And we know what a high percentage of them are coming back with medical issues. I put some 20 percent of them with traumatic brain injury. And we just have a responsibility in the totality of their financial situation to try put in place the kinds of programs that will help them and their families. And I thank you for this very important hearing.

The CHAIRMAN. Thank you, Senator Markey.

I'm still conflicted, OK? So you've got to help set me straight. Captain Alexander, I'm going to call you. You work with the Guard, you talk with the folks and they hear you, they believe you, but does it prepare them for these creeps that are going to descend on them? I mean, one's kind of a generalized warning and you hope they're listening and all the rest of it. But see, I'm torn between that approach and between getting all the attorney generals in the United States at one of their semi-annual—how many meetings do you have?

Mr. COOPER. We have one every late February/early March here in D.C., which would be perfect for that sort of discussion.

The CHAIRMAN. Well, I mean, I'm just torn between the whole kind of—and as I say that, I'm being rude, because you're working so hard, all of you, to get the word out and to educate people and to create stress so that they'll be alert and avoid some of these problems. But I keep coming back to what you said, and that is that they're kids. You used the word 22, 23, 24, 25; that's a kid, in terms of this kind of stuff. They haven't settled back out of the military and therefore into a neighborhood where they, in the course of being in that neighborhood, are warned by other people in that neighborhood who have been taken advantage of in certain ways so that they're alert, then. Because they're solid, they're rooted, they're at home and they're a different kind of receptor and might have a different kind of reaction. But you're trying to get to them and to reach out to them and to educate them.

On the other side is if the attorney generals, attorneys general—it took me a long time to learn that—all get together and you just pick out, you know, there's a whole bunch of smart guys in some of this testimony and you know they're out there. And again, we ran into the same thing in health insurance. They took advantage of anybody in any way that they could, just like the moving companies. Anybody they could get, they took advantage of. They're out there. They're not a secret.

Now, you indicated that you followed them around the country and everywhere that you went, they were there. Now, that's SmartBuy. That sounds like something that attorneys general could get together and say, you know, we've got ample evidence of what they've done and the troubles they've caused; let's clamp down on them, let's sue them, let's take them to court. Let's do an Ingenix on them. Because that will ring loud and clear. I think it will; I mean, they're maybe such small scumbag operations that they don't read the newspapers; they don't follow the Legal Times or whatever it is. They don't know what they're running into. But I'm just torn by it. I mean, each of them seems to be important and I have this need to come down on one side or the other and I think I'm probably wrong in that you have to do it both, but a lot of this is about outreach and education and I want to see some of it.

And General Cooper, you're already there. Assistant Attorney General Nelson, you're already there. You take people to court. And you know who they are. And you know what their track records are. Or, if you don't, you have your people do the research to find out who these little companies or semi-big companies or whatever they are, what they do. And you save all that time in the mess hall when people are sort of at peace and they're listening. But they still don't know what they're going to run into until they run into it. And then the outreach didn't work. Or, if you're lucky, the outreach did work and they were really bright and they picked up and took notes and, you know, held their own.

But I just don't think there's anything like setting examples when people are taken to court and get sued. And these companies lose. Now, in that case, the soldiers and sailors, men and women, don't necessarily know that, but you've cutoff the perpetrator. You've helped, or at least reduced, the power of the perpetrator and they become less aggressive. And I want you to help me understand those two philosophies and why it is that I'm sort of prejudice towards the more aggressive one but in so saying, I'm putting down one that absolutely has to happen, which is the outreach and the education. But, you know, I'm assuming that you know who the SmartBuys are. And you can go after them. Or am I wrong?

Captain ALEXANDER. Mr. Chairman, I think you have to have both.

If you educate the servicemember, they may still fall prey, but they can identify the issue, maybe after the fact. When in the military, we train and we train and then we do an engagement. For Consumer Law, there is no training except for life. You go out there and you live it and you pick up that this was bad and you don't do it again, hopefully. And so, we educate them. They may fall prey, but after that they can say, I know something was wrong here and they can call someone and tell them, then they can be the witnesses to bring the case that you want to bring.

I think you have to make an example also and I think the businesses do a cost-benefit analysis. They're going to look at something and say, I'm making lots of money, it's not costing me much risk. If you can increase the risk in that business balance sheet, then they're going to stop doing it or maybe find out a less harmful way of doing it. And that's something we need for the enforcement side.

The CHAIRMAN. Please. Ms. Nelson.

Ms. NELSON. If I may, Chairman; I think there's a third part of the solution that maybe needs to be mentioned here and that is, additional tools.

The attorneys general bringing lawsuits is something we enjoy doing, it's one of the exciting things when you can crack down on the bad guys and hopefully have some good effect. One of the things in this area though, sir, is that there are some lapses. We need some additional tools in our arsenal to be able to bring those types of cases and to be able to track those bad guys. Because frankly, all you need to become an unlicensed lender is a Xerox copy machine to copy off the new forms. They're very transient, very difficult to get a hold of. So a technical phrase that we use in the attorneys general field is "whack-a-mole."

[Laughter.]

Ms. NELSON. And it's, as soon as you crack down on one of these operators, you've got another one. When we shut down SmartBuy in New York state, a competitor in Oklahoma actually went and elbowed SmartBuy out of the mall there with these news articles and set up shop in that void. I think that an additional tool in that equation that you're formulating, education, enforcement, is also some stronger tools to track these unlicensed lenders, to have some registries so we can locate them quickly so we know who we're dealing with. Because frankly, many times the soldiers won't know they've been ripped off.

The CHAIRMAN. All right. Well then, let's say SmartBuy is pushed aside, as you say, in whatever state and somebody comes in and takes their place. Now, is that somebody who's completely off your radar screen?

Ms. NELSON. That's an excellent example, sir, and in that particular case, it was a business by the name of TECHsmart who came out as a California corporation with locations throughout the country, including in Georgia. My office contacted the Georgia Consumer Protection Bureau at the Governor's office and they took enforcement action against TECHsmart in Georgia; forced them out of Georgia. They're not in New York state at this point in time.

So one of the challenges that the state attorney generals would find is jurisdictional. We have states that we're responsible for and sometimes you're able to get a national hit on a case. For example, in SmartBuy, Integrity Financial of North Carolina, was one of the unlicensed lenders. As part of a negotiated settlement, we were able to cancel, cut down contracts nationally. That doesn't always happen.

The CHAIRMAN. How did you do that?

Ms. NELSON. It was a bargaining. It was fine negotiating——

The CHAIRMAN. A settlement?

[Laughter.]

Ms. NELSON. Yes.

The CHAIRMAN. All right. Well now, have you heard of this Military Financial? Have any of you heard of Military Financial? Because those are all the ads that I held up.

Ms. PETRAEUS. I'd just like to say, if you Google the term "military loans," which I did this afternoon shortly before I came over here, I got 72 million responses. And many of them are lenders on the Internet who use military or flag-waving, you know, in their advertisements. And a great many of them are outrageously expensive but they're like those ads that you held up. I won't speak to that particular company, but I can tell you there are an incredible number of them on the Internet. And it's very easy to put up a website and it's very easy to change your name of your company. So it's a scourge; we've got to educate people not to use them.

Some of them are outright scams, advanced fee scams, where you're told you have to put down a deposit to get the loan because your credit's not good. And once you send off that money, of course, you never hear from them again. And so we have to teach folks a red flag is always if somebody you don't know requires you to send money to them in advance for something they're going to do for you, that's most likely to be a bad thing. But these folks are very persuasive, it's what they do. And it's their model. And if they do get enforced against somewhere, they will go back to doing what they know how to do and they'll just do it in another state under another name.

So——

The CHAIRMAN. Do they tend to be companies of more than 10 or 12 people?

Ms. PETRAEUS. You know, it's hard to say. I remember one scam that was being run out of Kentucky when I was at the Better Business Bureau. It was actually offering to sell military ribbon racks, you know, that you put your decorations on, on your uniform? And that was just a guy and his girlfriend in a broken down old house somewhere in Kentucky. But they knew how to set up a nice website and they made a lot of money. So it doesn't take much.

Mr. COOPER. Mr. Chairman, if I could address your quandary?

The CHAIRMAN. Please.

Mr. COOPER. I would say that you do have to look at both elements of that equation: Education and enforcement. I would throw communication in there also. But enforcement needs to be diligent. It has a great deterrent effect and not only shuts down the particular company you're going after, it sends a signal to others in that business. But there are some drawbacks here. Keep in mind that our litigation with Rome/Britlee took 3 years to get to judgment, longer than that to actually collect on the judgment. By that point, particularly with regard to military personnel, accomplishing restitution was a challenge because a number of the people who perhaps had made these purchases between 2005 and prior had moved on.

Some of them were still in the military service; some of them were retired. It was a real challenge to track down those names. We found a lot of them with the help of the DOD and Fort Campbell and got the checks out, but it took a lot of effort. So, you know, it's not ideal just to focus on enforcement. You know, for those people, they would have been much better off had they kind of been educated up front and known to stay away from something like this.

You know, when they say education needs to start well before the soldier enlists with the Army or Navy or whichever branch of the service. In Tennessee, we're one of the few states where financial literacy training is a required part of the high school curriculum. Frankly, that's something that I'd like to see a greater number of states do. You have to get that training early so that, you know, when they find themselves moving into their career, you've got a base to build on. So that's a point I would make on that.

And then finally, communication. The AGs do work well together in all 50 states in sharing information. We have multi-state efforts in various consumer matters. We have recently created a working group specifically on military matters that will facilitate not just learning about what is going on in New York or Tennessee, but also where it crosses state lines to combine our efforts to go after that. And that is something that I think the AGs have a good track record on.

The CHAIRMAN. And that's helpful.

You know, there's another way that occurs to me, which is simply to embarrass. Frankly, that's one of the things that we will do from time to time on this committee because we have an investigations unit, we have subpoena power. And let's say SmartBuy, whatever 20 states they're in, et cetera, it's obviously not small. And you can send a U.S. Marshal to deliver a subpoena, right? I'm not a lawyer. So you have to say yes, I'm right, if I'm right.

[Laughter.]

Mr. COOPER. Yes, we can get subpoenas served.

The CHAIRMAN. Yes. OK. Or you get a couple of them and we have a hearing asking them to explain themselves. And you try really hard to get good press attendance. And you embarrass them; you take them out of the closet and then go after them. Now, let me ask you this question: If one were to do that, to say, SmartBuy, to ask them to come to a hearing, they would say, no. So you issue a subpoena and it's delivered. They could say, no? They couldn't. They could be in contempt, right?

Mr. COOPER. Yes.

The CHAIRMAN. See, I'm trying to find some way to get them to be seen as the scumbags that I think they are. And particularly when they, you know, have one name one day and another name the next day to stay ahead of whatever pursuit.

Mr. COOPER. Mr. Chairman, I think that a case like that would be a great case study and an opportunity to educate not just about that particular operation, but generally how these operations work.

The CHAIRMAN. Yes. Yes, exactly.

I don't know; it's hard. And you all work at it so hard, you know? I mean, it's something to really make an American citizen angry that this is happening. To those young men and women—or anybody, for that matter—and, you know, just as they're serving us, they're getting shafted under our watch in this country. Or if some of them get shafted when they're overseas, right? That can happen, too. There's just got to be a way somehow to combine our forces.

You can't do more outreach. I mean, you only have a certain number of people in education and that is going to work and there are going to be some smarter people that sort of fit into that and accept that and therefore are alerted to it and can stand up against it and ask the right questions and refuse to sign or whatever. But there's just nothing like the law. The power of an attorney general, I mean, in West Virginia, when I call it—Senator Thune, coming from an urban state, I tend to do that, I think he's rather tired of it, because West Virginia is, I think, even more rural than South Dakota. But an attorney general in West Virginia has vast power. And we have a lot of companies, including a lot of coal companies, who are evading this and doing that and attorney generals can do amazing things.

Well, I mean, I'm hearing what you're saying and I'm hearing that it has to be all of the above. So maybe we'd better not draw this out, but simply let me thank you for what you're doing. And please feel my frustration because I wasn't as familiar with this as I should have been until I prepared for this hearing. And I'm just absolutely outraged by it. And it would seem to be something that one could stop. The FTC, for heaven's sake; your organization, Ms. Petraeus; you know. Attorney general's office here in Washington; all the attorney generals gathered; plot strategies; I don't know. I don't know.

Anyway, it's a terrible thing to do to our men and women who serve us. And I regret it greatly. But what I do not regret at all is the five of you coming here today and giving your time to help educate us while this brain trust behind me, we'll go to work and try to see what we can come up with.

Is that OK, Mr. Harwood?

Mr. HARWOOD. The FTC would be happy to work with you on ideas in this area and hopefully we can come up with something that will be effective.

The CHAIRMAN. This has nothing to do with anything, but——

[Laughter.]

The CHAIRMAN.—do you know that in the Dodd-Frank Bill their intention was to get rid of the FTC?

Mr. HARWOOD. I heard that, yes.

The CHAIRMAN. Yes, well it was.

[Laughter.]

Mr. HARWOOD. I chose not to believe it, but I did hear it.

The CHAIRMAN. No, it was. And I had several conversations with Chris Dodd and he didn't want to do it, but then he became convinced that, because they were talking about putting your organization at that time down on the Federal Reserve Building. And as I drive by it, I just see a lawn. I mean, I don't know what they were going to do. So you fight to keep the FTC and Chris Dodd finally agreed, yes, it's better to have two sets of eyes rather than one set of eyes. Especially if one set isn't up and running yet.

But, gosh, we have to do something about this. And you are, and I'm just sitting here moaning that it happens at all. But such is life and such is our free enterprise system at the edges and we will persist. So this hearing is adjourned.

[Whereupon, at 4:17 p.m., the hearing was adjourned.]

APPENDIX

Prepared Statement of Michael S. Archer

To the Honorable Chairman, Commerce Committee, United States Senate

1. I am grateful for the opportunity to comment concerning the Military Lending Act (10 U.S.C. 987), the Servicemember Civil Relief Act (50 U.S.C. Appendix 501 et seq.), and other legislative matters concerning the financial protection of military servicemembers. In short, I believe that expansion of the protection afforded by the MLA is long overdue, and that changes to the SCRA are necessary, particularly concerning waiver, lease termination, and forced arbitration. I also suggest enhancements to consumer protection concerning abusive debt collection practices.

2. *My background.* Before moving on to more specific and detailed analysis, you should be aware that I have considerable experience in dealing with predatory lenders and others on a mission to separate servicemembers from their paycheck. I am a retired judge advocate, having served in the U.S. Marine Corps for twenty years, including four assignments as officer in charge of legal assistance: in Yuma, Arizona; Camp Lejeune, North Carolina, and twice in Okinawa, Japan. Under 10 U.S.C. 1044 and regulations promulgated by the Judge Advocate General of the Navy, the legal assistance section is directed to assist servicemembers and their dependents with civil legal matters and to conduct a consumer education and preventative law program. About two years after my military retirement, the billet of OIC Legal Assistance became a civilian position at Camp Lejeune, following a nationwide trend among all the armed forces. I was chosen to serve in that position in October 2004 and was then chosen to serve as the Regional Director of Legal Assistance for Marine Corps Installations East. I have been a member of the North Carolina State Bar standing committee on Legal Assistance for Military Personnel (NC LAMP) since 1995 and in 2006 I was honored to receive the State Bar's Distinguished Service Award for legal assistance to military personnel. In 2012, I received the Distinguished Service Award for Legal Assistance from the American Bar Association Committee on Legal Assistance for Military Personnel (ABA LAMP).

3. *Disclaimer.* My experiences as a Marine Officer, Judge Advocate, and Department of Defense civil servant over the past thirty years have been critical in the formation of my views concerning predatory lending and other consumer issues. Nonetheless, the views expressed herein are my own as a private citizen and do not necessarily represent the views of the Department of Defense, the Marine Corps or any of their respective instrumentalities.

The Military Lending Act

4. *The Military Lending Act, Overview*

In October 2006, Congress enacted the Military Lending Act (MLA) to ameliorate serious and persistent financial harm incurred by troops, particularly junior troops, resulting from unfair, deceptive, or abusive lending products. The MLA authorized the Secretary of Defense, within limitations, to regulate certain types of lending. The SECDEF exercised this authority very sparingly, covering only car title loans, refund anticipation loans, and payday loans, and even excluding some of them through narrowly drafted definitions (32 CFR 232). The senior attorney of each of the armed forces objected to this minimalist approach, recommending far more robust protections. In a joint letter dated August 29, 2007, the service JAGs recommended coverage of installment loans and rent-to-own transactions, as do I. In addition, with perfect 20/20 hindsight, I also recommend closing loopholes in existing protections that have been widely exploited by lenders to the detriment of our troops.

5. *The Military Lending Act and/or its implementing regulation should include payday loans, refund anticipation loans, car title loans, rent to own transactions, and installment loans regardless of whether the extension of credit is open ended or closed ended.*

a. The current law only addresses a subset of car title loans, refund anticipation loans, and payday loans. Such loans are only covered by the MLA if, in addition to other limitations concerning loan duration, they are considered closed ended credit. It seems to me that payday, car title and refund anticipation loans in excess of 36 percent, often in triple digit interest range, are inherently harmful and should be regulated by the MLA regardless of whether they are open or closed ended credit.

b. Over the past several years, I have seen schemes whereby lenders extend closed ended credit, but pretend that the transaction is open ended, thereby avoiding Truth in Lending Act (TILA) requirements to disclose the annual percentage rate of interest, total finance charges, and total expense after all the payments have been made. By the same expedient of simply labeling closed ended transactions as open ended, lenders can also evade the requirements of the MLA regulation to disclose to the borrower, orally and in writing (a) the annual percentage rate of interest, (b) any information required to be disclosed under TILA, and (c) a clear description of the payment obligations of the borrower. This practice of disguising closed ended transactions is particularly prone to involve service member credit transactions.

For example:

- Sellers of consumer electronics, targeting military servicemembers, finance the sale of a single transaction, fail to provide the consumer with any opportunity whatsoever for additional credit, and yet couch their contracts in terms of an open ended transaction. In some cases, young troops receive a letter from the lender after the transaction, revoking the supposed credit that they really never had in the first place.

- Sellers of a water filtration system solicit sales door to door in military towns, telling troops that the system costs a certain price, and that it can be paid off in three years. There is no opportunity whatsoever to make additional purchases with this so called open ended credit. The contracts for this discrete sale nonetheless state that they are for revolving (open ended) credit, give only a monthly percentage, and fail to provide the total interest, number of payments, or total cost, as would be required by TILA for close ended credit transactions.

- A Virginia car dealer charges 300 percent interest in auto purchase loans. The loan is structured, nominally, as open ended. Thus, even if the MLA were amended to include auto purchase loans, this particular loan would be excluded from coverage under current definitions because it is "open ended."

- Some banks have apparently decided to make payday loans to their depositors. In this scheme, after the designated time period, generally around ten days, the bank repays itself the principal and interest from the depositor's account. If the depositor does not have sufficient funds to make the required payment, the depositor is assessed a penalty as well. The customer can chose to borrow under such plans with the click of a button and with no disclosure whatsoever of rate or amount of interest. These transactions are generally immune from state regulation because the bank is either an out of state of national bank. These transactions are claimed to be open ended and thereby immune from the current MLA regulation.

c. Perhaps most importantly, we should not again underestimate the willingness or capacity of lenders to devise additional schemes to exclude more and more loans under existing regulations simply by calling transactions open-ended or by structural subterfuges designed to disguise essentially closed ended transactions as open ended.

6. *In crafting the next generation of lending restrictions under the MLA, we should not lose sight of payday lenders' demonstrated capacity for creative evasion.*

If history has taught us anything, it is that we can be certain that if there is any ambiguity, lack of enforcement, loophole, or wiggle room of any kind, payday lenders will take advantage of it to continue lending at interest rates that begin at around 390 percent. The sordid history of payday lending in North Carolina is a constructive lesson in lender deceit and evasion, summarized below.

- Prior to 1997, North Carolina had no law specifically addressing payday loans. In practice, payday lenders made two week loans at about 390 percent interest, marketing heavy to servicemembers and often located near military installations. An opinion of the North Carolina Attorney General of January 24, 1992 declared that payday loans were indeed loans, subject to the requirements of the North Carolina Consumer Finance Act which, among other things, prohibits the outrageous sort of interest rate characteristic of payday loans. Lenders ignored this opinion and continued to extend predatory payday loans unabated.

- Payday lenders used various ruses to pretend that their transactions were not loans. Some made the absurd assertion that they were simply cashing checks and not making loans at all, that all of their customers just so happened to write checks in the same denominations; *e.g.*, multiples of one hundred, and that in each case the 15–20 percent taken out was not a loan at all but rather a "fee" for this wonderful check cashing service supposedly paid willingly by idiots who chose to pay this exorbitant fee rather than use the free check cashing services on base or any of the convenient ATMs on or off base.
- Some payday lenders heavily advertised the delayed deposit feature, had business names suggesting that they provided loans, verbally told customers that they were lending money, required customers to provide the name and phone number of their commanding officers, and then extended a loan, but required all borrowers to sign a false statement indicating that they had sufficient funds in their account to cover the check . . . as if anyone in their right mind would pay 15 percent of the face value of a check just to cash it.
- Other lenders used a somewhat more elaborate ruse. They would sell telephone calling cards or some other trinkets to borrowers who wanted to cash checks at inflated rates. For example, a client would provide a $100 check and in exchange receive a phone card worth $15 (sold for $30), $70 cash, and a promise that the check would not be presented for payment until the next military payday (which occur every two weeks). These lenders would then claim that they didn't make any loans; they merely sold telephone calling cards. The payday lenders would have us believe that the fact that the card was overpriced in the amount of 15 percent of the face amount of the check, that every purchaser of phone cards voluntarily chose to write a check over the amount of the purchase, and that the phone card cost was always the same percentage of the check amount in every case.
- In 1997, North Carolina began an experiment concerning payday lending, authorizing the practice, but limiting the loan amount to a maximum of $300 and the interest rate to 15 percent of the face value of the loan. The NC Commissioner of Banks was directed to report on payday lending. In the absence of further legislative approval, payday lending was set to expire July 31, 2001. The February 22, 2001 Banking Commission report to the General Assembly reported 8,911 violations of various aspects of the payday lending law by licensees and found ten unlicensed payday lenders. Of course, consumers were harmed, as they always are, by loans at excessive interest rates, regardless of whether the practice is lawful.
- After the North Carolina law authorizing payday lending was allowed to sunset, payday lending continued in the state practically unabated. In addition to reverting to the pre-legislation schemes, payday lenders entered into dubious and tenuous relationships with out of state banks as a means of evading state regulation. It took several actions (and several years) by the North Carolina Attorney General and the North Carolina Commissioner of Banks to thwart these schemes.
- In recent years, payday lenders have been knocking on the statehouse doors again, pushing for legislation that would authorize payday lending. In an attempt to placate military interests, some of these proposals suggested exclusion of payday loans to servicemembers and their families. The North Carolina Commanders' Council, comprised of every installation commander in the state, unanimously rejected this approach. In a letter dated March 11, 2013, the NCCC wrote that "The Council does not opposed S89 [NC Senate bill authorizing payday lending] merely because of its inconsistency with Federal law. We believe that any law authorizing payday lending in this state will make the extension of such credit to our troops, their dependents, and the greater military community more likely. Further, we do not underestimate the established ingenuity of payday lenders to exploit loopholes in state and Federal laws."

7. *The MLA and its implementing regulation should apply to rent-to-own (RTO) purchases.*

In a joint letter to the Secretary of Defense, the Judge Advocates General of every branch of the armed forces ("Implementation of Section 670 of the FY 2007 NDAA," Memorandum for Under Secretary of Defense for Personnel and Readiness, dated 29 August 2007) recommended that the MLA implementing regulation be reviewed to "implement all of the financial protections for servicemembers and their dependents contemplated by [the MLA]." These senior military legal advisors specifically recommended that the regulations include RTO transactions and installment loans, products identified by the Department of Defense to be particularly problematic (along with payday loans, car title loans, and refund anticipation loans). The American Bar Association voiced similar concerns. (ABA Govt Affairs Office Acting Director Denise A Cardmon ltr June 11, 2007)

By and large, RTO presents lenders with an opportunity to charge triple digit interest, for the purchase of used property, all without disclosing any aspect of interest charged, including rates and without any equity established by the consumer's periodic payments. RTO customers rent furniture, consumer electronics, or other property and, after a designated number of months, may purchase the property by paying an additional fee. When all of the costs are added up, the consumer winds up paying far more than if the purchase had been made outright, and even more than if the purchase had been made with a credit card or a high interest installment loan. If evaluated as interest, these extra costs amount to extraordinarily high interest, far in excess of that authorized by the MLA. The Maryland Attorney General provided the following examples: If a $400 washing machine were purchased on an 18 month installment plan at the maximum authorized interest in that state (24 percent APR) the total cost to the consumer would be $480. The same transaction made under a typical 18 month RTO plan, would cost over a thousand dollars more, and it might even be for a used machine! In another example, a Maryland consumer purchased a used computer with a cash price of $649. But by making the purchase though an RTO contract calling for 52 weekly payments, the price skyrocketed to $1,364. "Rent to Own: Worth the Convenience?" Maryland Attorney General on line January/February 2003, last accessed July 22 2013. *http://www.oag.state.md.us/consumer/edge109.htm*

Not only is the consumer charged extraordinary interest, without any interest disclosures, but the property may be repossessed and sold. Furthermore, unlike with straight financing of the sale, the RTO repossession and sale will proceed without any reimbursement, credit, or consideration at all of the consumer's monthly "rent" payments, which do not establish any owner equity in the property.

Make no mistake about it, most RTO transactions are loans. Between December 1998 and February 1999, the Federal Trade Commission surveyed 500 RTO customers and found that 70 percent ultimately purchased the property. ("Survey of Rent-to-Own Customers: Federal Trade Commission Bureau of Economics Staff Report," James M. Lacko, Signe Mary McKernan, and Manoj Hastak April 2000)

The MLA exempts from its coverage, "a loan procured in the course of purchasing a car or other personal property when that loan is offered for the express purpose of financing the purchase and is secured by the car or personal property procured." RTO vendors may attempt to claim that they fit within this exemption. However, Congress never intended to exempt RTO. As the Service JAGs noted, the MLA was based on the August 9, 2006 Department of Defense Report to Congress, which identified five predatory practices, including RTO. Furthermore, the RTO is significantly different in character than exempted purchase money security agreement. It is not a loan for the "express purpose" of financing a purchase; rather, it has the additional feature of rental payments. The initial payments are rent and not installment payments; they do not establish any consumer equity, and there is no obligation to make a purchase. How convenient for RTO vendors to insist that the RTO transaction is not a loan for the purpose of TILA (thus avoiding its mandatory disclosures), but that RTO is a loan (with the property as security) for the purposes of the MLA. In any event, the MLA is hardly a model of clarity concerning its treatment of RTO transactions and should be amended to make it clear that RTO transactions are included within its coverage.

8. *RTO stores should be specifically prohibited from renting or selling computers or any other consumer electronics that spy on the purchaser/buyer.*

Basic fairness and common sense dictate that when you rent or purchase a computer, the seller should not be using the computer to photograph consumers, obtain personal information, and log the consumer's keystrokes, all without consumer knowledge or consent. Yet this is precisely what seven RTO companies did, at least until they were caught and sanctioned by the Federal Trade Commission. "FTC Approves Final Order Settling Charges Against Software and Rent to Own Companies Accused of Computer Spying," FTC News Release April 15, 2013 *http://www.ftc.gov/opa/2013/04/designerware.shtm*

Inclusion of such a prohibition in the MLA implementing regulation, with serious civil and criminal penalties for the violation thereof, will stand as clear and unambiguous warning and deterrent to RTO stores (which apparently need such motivation) and will provide servicemembers with an additional and more efficient remedy then currently exist. Furthermore, not only do servicemembers deserve such heightened protection, but national security demands it. The opportunity for RTO stores and their partners to gather intelligence data and to blackmail troops via computer spying should not be ignored.

9. *The MLA should apply to installment loans.*

As noted by the service JAGs, the August 2006 Department of Defense Report to Congress military identified installment loans as a problem transaction. Both the JAGs and the ABA expressed concern about its exclusion from the original implementation regulation.

Installment lenders market high cost loans to troops. For example:

- A car title lender charges 400 percent interest, but has a 32 month payback period, thus evading the MLA because the duration of the loan exceeds the definition of a car title loan. It is therefor an installment loan, unregulated by the MLA.
- A South Carolina lender whose name indicates that it is specifically targeting troops, charges 80 percent interest, requires payment via military allotment (and authorization for bank draft if the allotment fails for any reason), and requires "consent" to contact the borrowers command Its contracts claim that Delaware law applies. This installment loan is not addressed by the MLA.
- Another lender, operating on-line, charges 359 percent interest and claims that the law of the Chippewa Tribe of Montana applies. These loans are installment loans exempt from MLA coverage.
- Another lender whose name indicates that it is specifically marketing to troops, charges 80 percent interest and claims that the law of Nevada (no state usury statute) applies. The lender requires payment via payroll allotment, with bank draft authority if the allotment fails. The loan contract also purports to waive the protections of the SCRA. The payback period is 12 months; ergo, it is an installment loan exempt from MLA coverage.
- A lender outside Ft Hood, Texas charges over 580 percent APR, requires payment every two weeks, but has a loan period in excess of 90 days and is therefore considered an installment loan, outside the ambit of MLA coverage.

In addition to evasion of the MLA by virtue of being installment loans, many lenders use choice of law and venue provisions in their contracts purporting to invoke the law of an anti-consumer state rather than the state in which the borrower, the lender, and the transaction are actually located. The difficulty of enforcing state law is made even more complicated if the loan in made on line. Thus, the law of the least consumer friendly states may be exported to the rest of the country. Coverage of installment loans by the MLA can help stop this race to the bottom.

Installment loan products are often sold in conjunction with additional high cost, low value products such as collateral insurance, credit life insurance, and disability insurance. The typical sale involves the lender's agent preparing a contract including all of products, which are also financed at the high contract APR. As a practical matter, in the face of these tactics, lender salesmanship, and consumer desperation, it takes a savvy junior troop to opt out of these add—ons. When the purchase of these products is folded into the cost of the loan, their cost should be included in calculating the military annual percentage rate (MAPR) of interest.

If purchase of these or any other add on products is not required as a condition of obtaining credit, the consumer should be advised by clear and conspicuous disclosures, separate from the loan contract, that purchase of the add on is not required to obtain credit or to obtain credit at the contract rate.

In any event, lenders should be prohibited from selling disability insurance to troops in connection with installment loans, particularly short term loans (two years or less). The purpose of disability insurance is to secure monthly payments in the event that the borrower is injured so badly that he cannot work and therefore loses employment income. This rationale makes no sense in the context of a military borrower, who will continue to be paid despite injury, and if discharged medically from the armed forces (generally a very lengthy process, during which he will receive full pay) he will likely be entitled to either a severance pay or a monthly disability payment from the Department of Veteran's Affairs.

9. *Debt Collection: Covered commercial creditors should be prohibited from contacting commanders and other third parties absent written permission by the debtor given after default.*

One of the reasons that troops are targeted for predatory loans is the perception, and the reality, that they can be manipulated into compliance with unreasonable demands by threats to contact their military superiors. The Federal Fair Debt Collection Practices Act (15 U.S.C. 1601 et seq.) already prohibits debt collectors from providing debt information to third parties, such as employers. North Carolina law contains similar prohibitions against debt collection agencies; *i.e.,* those in the business of collecting debts for others (NC Gen Stat 58–7–1 through 130), but wisely goes further and applies this principal to commercial creditors collecting their own debts (NC Gen Stat 75–50 through 56). NC commercial creditors are prohibited from providing debt information to third parties absent consumer consent given *in writing after default*. Such purported consent to contact commanders, provided in credit applications and other documents prior to default, is void and of no effect. Debt collection threats and harassment is harmful to troops whether perpetrated by debt collectors or creditors, and both be covered by the MLA.

Service members are vulnerable to such threats because such contact can sour the critical relationship between troop and superior, and troops may perceive, in some cases rightly so, that creditor complaints, even if inaccurate, may adversely affect subjective performance and conduct ratings, assignment, reenlistment, and promotion decisions, and may even result in disciplinary action. The MLA should, like NC law, prohibit such debt collection contact with third parties, thereby extending the protection to all states. In addition, such fine tuning of the MLA can help prevent lenders from evading state debt collection law by the artifice of contractually citing another state's law as governing.

Lenders in military towns often require loan applicants to execute written consent to provide debt collection information to military authorities. Not only should such contact be prohibited, but the practice of even asking for pre-default consent should be clearly prohibited as well. Such written consent, even if void and ineffective as a matter of law, is a veiled threat, giving the false impression that such command contact is authorized. These bogus consent provisions are nearly ubiquitous in military lending contracts, even in states that declare such pre default consent void.

10. *The MLA should prohibit unreasonable choice of venue provisions.*

At least one creditor selling products near Camp Lejeune, North Carolina and other military installations, heavily markets to service members has a choice of venue provision in its standard contract requiring any lawsuit by the creditor or the borrower must be initiated in Virginia, notwithstanding that the parties and the transaction are all in North Carolina. This business sells various products in which it takes a security interest, and is therefore exempt from the MLA. Such a contractual provision likely does not actually deprive North Carolina jurisdiction, which is governed by its long arm statute (NC Gen Stat 1–75.4). However, such contractual language provides an additional hurdle for military litigants to overcome. More importantly, such a provision serves as a deterrent to unsophisticated troops (and for that matter, unsophisticated attorneys) from bringing meritorious cases before the local courts. With litigation costs and rigorous, dangerous, and time consuming military duties already serving as barriers to the courtroom, lenders should be prohibited from further sealing the door on litigation tighter with contracts that purport to require that cases be initiated in some state distant from the borrower. Nor should creditors be allowed to initiate litigation against military consumers in distant, inconvenient states where it is more difficult to respond.

11. *The MLA should cover payday, RTO, refund anticipation loans, installment loans, and vehicle title loans regardless of the duration of the loan.*

The short duration of MLA covered loans is an important factor in making them difficult for borrowers to repay. However, a far more important factor in making these loans harmful is their exorbitant interest. The regulation should be amended to prevent lenders from evading the MLA interest cap by adjusting the duration of the loan. Under the current regulation, a payday loan of 91 days or less is covered; a payday loan of 92 days or more is not covered. A vehicle title loan of 181 days is covered; a vehicle title loan of 182 days is not. These provisions should be amended to cover all payday and title loans regardless of duration. Likewise, RTO and installment loan interest should be limited by the MLA regardless of the duration of the loan.

The Servicemember Civil Relief Act

13. *SCRA Overview.* The Soldiers and Sailors Civil Relief Act, amended and renamed the Servicemember Civil Relief Act (SCRA) in 2003, has long protected troops from financial harm at home as they tend to the Nation's defense. The SCRA has had an equally long history of revisions found necessary in the light of experience. To cite just a few examples, the SCRA was amended, twice, to include protection concerning wireless telephone service contracts, unheard of by the original drafters of the World War II era legislation. Another change, the specific, statutory enshrinement of a private and public right of action to enforce the SCRA, was enacted in direct response to Federal litigation in Michigan. Evasions and attempted evasions by lenders and other businesses resulted in still other amendments; for example: addition of language requiring lenders to forgive, and not just to defer, excess interest on loans covered by SCRA section 527. Likewise, section 535 has undergone multiple changes, some of them to reign in landlord evasions, first by pro-

viding that the troop's termination of his lease obligations also terminated his spouse's obligations, and later to provide that in the notice to quit, written verification of qualifying orders by the commander was a sufficient substitute for the production of military orders themselves. The SCRA has often had to be amended in the light of changed circumstances and experience; such is the case once again.

14. *SCRA Section 535 should be expanded to authorize lease termination in the event of the service member's death.*

Section 535 of the SCRA provides that a military tenant has the right to terminate a residential lease early if the lease was entered into prior to military service or the lease was entered into while on active duty and the service member thereafter receives orders to deploy, or the service member signs the lease while on active duty and thereafter receives orders to go to a new duty station. It does NOT provide for any lease termination rights in the event that the service member is killed. The grieving widow is stuck trying to find another renter in order to mitigate damages or paying the rent through the end of the lease term. When I proposed such an amendment to the NC General Assembly, the law passed unanimously in both houses and was signed by the Governor on June 26, 2012 [NC House Bill 971, 2011–12 legislative session codified as NC Gen Stat 42-45(a)(3)]. Of course, this North Carolina legislation has no effect in the other 49 states.

15. *The SCRA 535 definition of Permanent Change of Station (PCS) orders should be tied to the military definition of PCS orders.*

Section 535 of the SCRA, as noted above, provides a right to terminate a lease early in the event that a civilian tenant thereafter becomes a member of the armed forces, or a military tenant receives deployment or permanent change of station (PCS) orders. But what orders exactly does PCS include? Certainly, it includes orders from Camp Lejeune, North Carolina to Camp Pendleton, California as the term PCS is commonly used. But does it include orders upon retirement or release from active duty? The Joint Federal Travel Regulations (JFTR) at section U5000, which govern this matter within the armed forces, defines PCS orders to include all of these items. Accordingly, these types of orders should, likewise, give rise to lease termination authority under SCRA section 535, which was the position taken by the U.S. Department of Justice in the case of *U.S. v Empirian Property Management, Inc.* (D. Nebraska, March 8, 2012), which settled in favor of all the tenants. However, the U.S. DOJ does not have the resources to sue to enforce this position on every landlord that doesn't want to let a service member out of his/her lease in accordance with the law and uses the lack of a definition of PCS in SCRA section 535to the detriment of service members. Why not therefore import the definition of PCS Orders at SCRA section 535 to the definition found in the pertinent military regulation?

16. *SCRA 535 should authorize a right to residential lease termination upon the service member's acceptance of government quarters on the installation.*

Upon receipt of orders to their new duty station, troops may find, as I did during my career, that there is a waiting list to get into base quarters. Accordingly, service members obtain private rental quarters outside the installation. However, it is exceedingly unlikely that base quarters will become available precisely at the time that the off base residential lease expires, resulting in a difficult choice for the service member. Moving onto the installation allows the service member to enjoy its myriad advantages: decent housing, DOD Schools, better security, nearby medical care, child care, physical fitness and recreational facilities; a responsible landlord, and avoidance of the twice daily crush of traffic traversing the installation gate. However, taking advantage of the opportunity to live on base generally requires the service member to breach the existing residential lease, risking liability for paying rent through the remainder of the lease term if another renter is not found. SCRA section 535 should authorize lease termination for taking base quarters, thereby relieving the service member of this dilemma. Virginia law provides some protection in this regard, authorizing lease termination if the service member is ordered to base quarters (VA Code Ann 55–248.21:1). Florida law is even better and should serve as a model, providing such protection in the event that the service member is ordered to government quarters or if he voluntarily elects government quarters, the more typical situation (FL Stat 83: 682).

17. *The SCRA should prohibit forced arbitration in contracts with service members.*

Increasingly, important financial transactions are characterized by the consumer's waiver of the right to trial and the right to participate in a class action lawsuit, in favor of arbitration. The arbitration is "forced," in the sense that the party with all the bargaining power writes the contract and the consumer is forced into it as a condition of making the transaction. You want to finance, or even purchase, a car, you need to "agree" to give up your day in court. It is easy to predict the expansion of forced arbitration, say to leases, mortgages, credit cards, all forms of consumer credit, and other consumer transactions.

Setting aside for the moment the questions of arbitrator bias in favor of the large corporation for whom he is dependent on additional business, and the over all fairness of forced arbitration, the practice also effectively causes the service member to give up many of his rights under the SCRA, which applies to "any judicial or administrative proceeding commenced in any [civil] court or agency in any jurisdiction subject to this Act (SCRA section 512b). It does not apply to arbitration.

The most basic protection that service members possess under the SCRA is the protection against losing in court because military duties prevent him from showing up. The SCRA requires the plaintiff to assert the military status of the defendant, and provides that military defendant some protection against default judgments, the right to reopen erroneously entered default judgments, and the right to delay proceedings as military exigencies require. Such SCRA protections are inapplicable to arbitration.

Lenders, particularly car dealers, are apt to extol the virtues of arbitration as a means of resolving disputes without the costs associated with trial. I have my doubts concerning the fairness and supposed efficiencies of arbitration. In addition, the class action lawsuit may be the only effective remedy when many consumers are harmed, but the amount in dispute in any individual case does not practically justify individual action. However, assuming, arguendo, that arbitration is indeed a fair and efficient means of resolving consumer disputes, prohibition *of forced* arbitration would not stop parties from entering into a more voluntary agreements after the dispute arises, rather than as a condition in the original contract.

I also find it particularly instructive that when auto manufacturers imposed arbitration on auto dealers as a condition of obtaining a franchise, the auto dealers complained of the unfairness of this practice and successfully lobbied Congress for a special exemption, the Motor Vehicle Franchise Contract Fairness Act [15 U.S.C. 1226(a)(2)]. The same auto dealers now routinely impose on their consumers what they themselves viewed as intolerable.

18. *The SARA should not be waivable.*

SCRA section 517 provides that it may be waived, so long as the waiver is in writing, is executing during or after the service member's military service, is executed in an instrument separate from the obligation to which it applies, and is in at least 12 point type. Thus, members can sign away protections concerning foreclosure, repossession, residential leases termination, default judgments, interest rate limitations, delays in civil hearings, protection of insurance, etc. This "voluntary" stripping of all SCRA rights in contracts of adhesion imposed on unsophisticated and relatively powerless troops should be prevented by prohibiting waiver of SCRA rights by the parties.

Debt Collection

19. The Far Debt Collection Practices Act (15 U.S.C. 1692 et seq.) should apply to commercial creditors collecting their own debts as well as debt collectors hired to collect the debts of others. Why do we prohibit debt collectors to abuse and harass consumers but allow commercial creditors to do so? North Carolina has separate statutes prohibiting debt collection abuse from debt collection agencies and consumer creditors, NC Gen Stat 58–70–1 et seq., and NC Gen Stat 75–50 et seq., respectively. If this approach is not deemed politically feasible, perhaps a more narrow approach may be taken, for example, prohibiting commercial creditors from contacting the obligor's military superiors.

20. Contacting the debtor's military supervisors for the purpose of collecting a debt, threatening to do so, or providing contractual, pre-default "consent" to do so should be specifically prohibited.

Again, I offer my sincere thanks for the opportunity to offer comments and suggestions on these important matters concerning the welfare of our troops.

PREPARED STATEMENT OF THE NATIONAL INDEPENDENT AUTOMOBILE DEALERS ASSOCIATION (NIADA)

Mr. Chairman and Members of the Committee, my name is Steve Jordan, Executive Vice President of the National Independent Automobile Dealers Association (NIADA) with headquarters in Arlington, Texas. On behalf of the Association, I appreciate the opportunity to submit this statement for the record regarding the Committee's November 20th hearing on "Soldiers as Consumers: Predatory and Unfair Business Practices Harming the Military Community."

The National Independent Automobile Dealers Association represents more than 17,000 members who are connected to the automobile industry in some form or fashion, but primarily independent dealers who own dealerships across America that are not affiliated with a manufacturer.

They are businessmen and women who subscribe to a code of ethics that emphasizes honor, integrity and fair dealing. More than 40 percent of these dealers have been in business for more than 20 years, and almost 50 percent have five or fewer employees. They are the small car store that survives in the best of times and the worst of times because they are a part of their communities as fathers, mothers, Better Business Bureau members, Chamber of Commerce members, city councilmen, school board members, churchgoers, youth organization sponsors and coaches, and task force members who look for ways to make our cities and our towns better places to live.

If they are fortunate enough to have a military installation near their business, they strive to reach out and include the active personnel and the veterans who call our communities home. The military residents in turn volunteer for Special Olympics, literacy councils that provide free tutoring, school field days and Relay for Life, to name just a few.

NIADA's leadership is committed to these service members *and* the citizens within the communities they represent. Our mission states that as a not-for-profit organization we will "anticipate, recognize and respond to current and future issues and needs of the independent motor vehicle industry *and* the consumer." The NIADA Foundation's goal goes further by pledging "to improve the used motor vehicle industry by informing consumers, educating dealers and training individuals and companies associated with the industry."

NIADA stands ready to use our current resources, including our education and training staff, state association directors—many of whom are veterans—and our Automotive Consumer Television Network, which is available to anyone via the Internet at *http://niadatv.com/autoconsumer/*, to address the needs of car-buying military personnel—active or retired.

In that regard we have produced a simple to understand video that explains the car-buying process for active service members or those returning to civilian life. The video, "Car Buying Tips for Military Service Members," is available for viewing on Automotive Consumer Television, our Internet TV network providing industry information and education for consumers, as well as NIADA.TV and NIADA.com.

It is similar to the one NIADA produced several years ago targeting the teenager buying his/her first car.

Additional service member oriented plans include coordinating a speakers bureau with our state associations, tapping local dealers who will serve as resources to conduct safe car-buying seminars for local military installations, and providing NIADA education and training staff that will work with state associations in addressing proper military protocol at military installations.

In addition, I am enclosing some specific examples of the ways our members have been responsive and helpful to the military community, as follows:

From a dealer in North Carolina:

"We give all active military a $500 discount on any vehicle in our inventory. In 21 years I don't remember any negative situations with JAG. In fact, I have been involved in a couple of situations to try and help resolve problems soldiers were having with other businesses. We have supported various military charities, events, families and especially those serving overseas. We strictly adhere to the Servicemembers Civil Relief Act (SCRA). In fact, we have had several situations where service members have requested relief under the Act and were not covered according to the SCRA. However, we accommodated their requests even though we had no obligation to do so (that has included reducing their rate as well as the early termination of a lease). We welcome soldiers to bring in their SGT and/or 1st SGT when discussing the terms of their financing."

From a dealer in California:

"There was a customer who went to Afghanistan. He wanted to sell his car, a Toyota RAV4, but he didn't have time to do it. He left it here and told me what he wanted for it. I sold it a week or 10 days later and deposited the money into his account. He got back to me and said he got it and said thank you very much. Another guy who went to Afghanistan, he had bought a truck from me. When they go overseas, they have to park their cars somewhere on the base, and they have to pay a minimum of $100 a month for a storage fee. He told me he didn't want to pay $100, so I said,

'OK, leave it with us.' So we kept it on our lot. Every other day we'd start the car to make sure it was running, we kept it charged up, we washed it. When he got back the car was running and in good shape."

From Vets-Cars:

"Vets-Cars, an association of auto dealers whose mission is to help veterans, military personnel and their families in the car-buying process. Vets-Cars includes about 200 dealers in 25 states, among them several NIADA members. "We ask the dealers to pledge to our code of conduct as to how they are going to treat military car buyers. Everything has to be transparent and up front. There's a famous quote from Theodore Roosevelt: "A man who's willing to shed his blood for his country should be offered a fair and square deal afterward." And that's pretty much the bedrock of our association. And we monitor our dealers. We make sure they're doing the right things. We have on our website what we call the "After Action Report"—a customer satisfaction survey. Our agreement with our dealers specifically states two or more unresolved issues with veteran or military buyers and we can't have them in our program."

From a dealer in Texas:

"Some of the things I do for the military—most of the time, their issues are with the down payment. So I'll do a deferred down payment for them. Maybe I'll let them put 50 percent down and hold the car and let them make payments on the down payment until they get what they need to take possession of the vehicle. I vouch for some of them with sub-prime credit lenders—I'll let them take the vehicle and let the finance company know that I'll back it up for the first couple of months. I have soldiers come to me for advice on purchasing a vehicle whether they're buying it from me or not. I try to point them in the right direction. A lot of soldiers come to me for advice, since I'm a retired 1st Sgt. and I get a lot of recommendations. They come down here and talk to me. I tell them, first of all, buy something you want. Don't buy something somebody's pushing you into just to make a sale. They respect that. A lot of them purchase vehicles from me and some don't, but I still advise them."

From another dealer in California:

"There are a lot of individual cases. For example, a military guy came in to try to trade in a Jetta. The reason he wanted to trade it in was because it didn't run. He had bought it from someone else. So we're like, "Dude, you know we can't do anything for you. But I'll tell you what I will do. Why don't you bring it to our shop and we'll go ahead and fix your car for you and we won't charge you." There are a lot of things like that. It happens all the time. We stored a car for eight months for a soldier who couldn't pay $100 a month for storage—we kept his battery charged, kept his truck running. We've consigned cars for them and deposited the money in their account when they were in Afghanistan. We've sold their cars for them. We're the poster child for supporting the military in the used car business."

In closing, NIADA stands ready to assist all service members, including those returning to civilian life, and the Senate Commerce Committee any way we possibly can.

Thank you.

RESPONSE TO WRITTEN QUESTIONS SUBMITTED BY HON. AMY KLOBUCHAR TO DEANNA R. NELSON

Question 1. Ms. Nelson, you mentioned that soldiers are more vulnerable than other consumer groups because of their regular paychecks and allotments as well as their fear of disciplinary action for challenging a collection or stopping an allotment. What more can we do to deter bad actors from targeting soldiers? What further action should Congress take?

Answer. These are excellent questions, Senator Klobuchar. Because soldiers are often between a rock and a hard place—having provided automatic payments and also being duty—bound to maintain financial good standing—steps to provide some space between are needed to even the playing field. There are legislative steps which would assist soldiers in these situations.

One would be to strengthen the Federal Servicemembers Civil Relief Act and the Fair Debt Collection Practices Act to prohibit creditors as well as third—party debt collectors from contacting a soldier's chain of command with regard to a debt unless that debt has been reduced to judgment, and proper protocol is followed. At present there is nothing in the Servicemembers Civil Relief Act which protects soldiers from direct pursuit by nefarious creditors. Further the FDCPA does not extend its protections to individuals being harassed by creditors themselves—only third party debt collectors. By broadening the definition of a "debt collector" to any creditors, soldiers and all consumers would be afforded additional protection from these predators which have learned that by contacting a soldier's chain of command they dramatically increase their leverage for payment of disputed debts.

Another measure would be to prohibit reporting a soldier's alleged debt to a credit reporting agency unless the soldier has been given notice and debt has been reduced to judgment. There is a lot of abuse of the credit reporting system as a debt collection tool, particularly with soldiers who move frequently and many times are unaware of action taken against them in local courts, or are unable to comply with forum selection clauses in contracts. Similarly, many times the first notice a soldier has of an alleged debt is by reviewing a credit report. Unfortunately, a negative credit report can have disastrous impact upon a soldier's security clearance or position in the military even where the debt itself is questionable.

A third consideration would be to take a hard look at the military allotment payment system to evaluate its need in a modern society where soldiers now have access to several methods of auto pay. Allotment payments do not protect soldiers the way credit card or even debit card payments do, for example, there is no recourse for the soldier if a payment is disputed. At minimum, prohibiting businesses and individuals from contractually requiring payment by allotment would be a step forward.

By increasing the accountability of our soldiers' business partners, we can level the playing field and increase the fairness to servicemembers.

Question 2. Ms. Nelson, in the case of products being sold to soldiers through financing plans, businesses should be required to be transparent about the retail value of the product so that the consumer knows what he or she should be paying. How can states or the Federal government better protect soldiers and consumers, perhaps by requiring transparency at purchase?

Answer. At present, Senator Klobuchar, there is no legislation which compels retailers to disclose the MSRP of most classes of consumer goods. It is therefore easier to hide large mark ups over the typical retail price. Disclosure of the actual MSRP or average retail selling price would make these deceptive sales easier for a consumer to spot.

○